麗質華堂

王世襄題

中国紫檀博物馆

陈丽华 编著

文物出版社

封面题字：王世襄
书籍设计：特木热
摄　　影：孙之常
　　　　　刘小放
责任印制：梁秋卉
责任编辑：张小舟

图书在版编目（CIP）数据

丽质华堂：中国紫檀博物馆 / 陈丽华编著. -- 增订本. -- 北京：文物出版社，2013.6
ISBN 978-7-5010-3725-4

Ⅰ. ①丽… Ⅱ. ①陈… Ⅲ. ①紫檀－博物馆－介绍－中国②紫檀－木家具－收藏－中国－图集③紫檀－木雕－收藏－中国－图集 Ⅳ. ① G268.8 ② G894-64

中国版本图书馆 CIP 数据核字 (2013) 第 106097 号

麗質華堂
——中国紫檀博物馆
陈丽华 编著

文物出版社出版发行
北京东直门内北小街 2 号楼
http://www.wenwu.com
E-mail: web@wenwu.com
北京金彩印刷有限公司印刷
2013 年 6 月第 1 版　2013 年 6 月第 1 次印刷
635×965　1/8　印张：38.25
ISBN 978-7-5010-3725-4
定价：380.00 元

丽质华堂

中国紫檀博物馆

编辑委员会

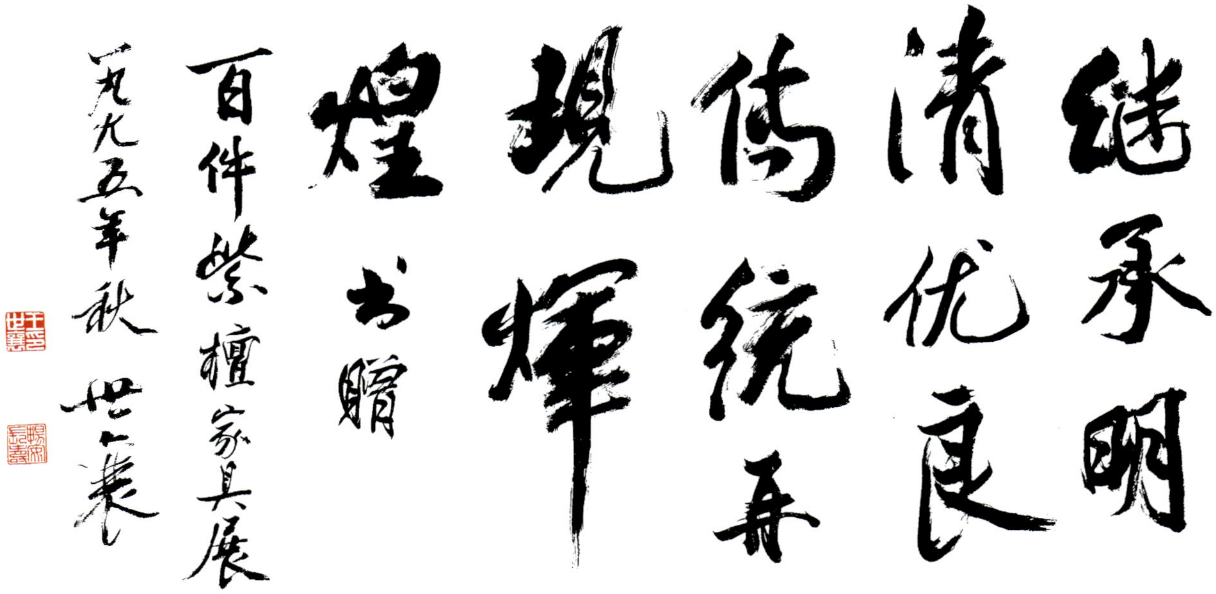

王世襄 题词 Inscription by Mr. Wang Shixiang

良匠造器妙巧
應規俯仰灼照
商畧神奇假物
興思須以忘疲

麗華女士屬為富華公司所製器題詞乃錄音人隱几銘朱家溍

朱家溍 题词 Inscription by Mr. Zhu Jiajin

目录

紫云清风

金丝绝唱

乌衣门第

屏风清影

古建余晖

匠意玲珑

王世襄
中国文物研究所研究员
中央文史馆馆员

by Mr. Wang Shixiang
Research Fellow of Research Institute of Chinese Culture Heritage of the State Bureau of Cultural Relics
Member of Central Research Institute of Culture and History

前言

紫檀早在公元三世纪，就经晋崔豹作为珍贵木材写入《古今注》。张彦远《历代名画记》述及唐内府用紫檀作轴头，以为非此不足以装配书法名画。宋赵汝适《诸蕃记》讲到紫檀，得知当时的主要产地不在本土，而在东南亚诸国。元大都延春阁内有紫檀御榻，见陶宗仪的《辍耕录》。明王佐《格古要论》将紫檀定为“异木”，意即“珍异之木”。以上记载足以说明紫檀自古以来一直受到特别的重视，位居各种珍贵木材之首。

紫檀珍贵固有其质色之美好绝伦，而产地偏远，生长缓慢，成材极难也是其重要原因。宋元以前的紫檀器物除唐时已运往日本，有幸保存在日本正仓院的几件棋局、小架外，竟难举出更多的实例。明中叶以后，拓展南疆，开放海禁，才有少量紫檀制成的家具。其中得以传至今日的早已成为稀世之珍。

清王朝统一中国后，直到雍正年间紫檀家具制作始渐具规模。鼎盛时期则在乾隆年代。弘历帝耽爱器物陈设。能工巧匠殚精竭思，历时数十载才制造出数量可观，在历史上占有特殊地位的所谓“贡作”紫檀家具。可惜仅此一朝，其后难以为继，随着国运衰落，家具也每况愈下了。

紫檀家具是中华的瑰宝，民族的骄傲。陈丽华女士对此有深刻的认识，由衷的爱好，故以继承、发展这一传统工艺为己任。她不惜耗费巨资，搜购良材，延请名匠，以故宫珍藏为典范，精工雕制，尽力倾心，孜孜不倦，竟达到忘我的程度。十余年来集中工匠数百人，营建厂房几十楹，制成精品逾千件，规模成就除乾隆内府外，可谓绝无仅有。为了妥善保管传之久远，供广大人民参观欣赏，借鉴研究，特修建这座美仑美奂的紫檀家具博物馆。此举不云绝后，确是空前。相信各位观众从本馆可以看到陈丽华女士热爱祖国文化，为弘扬中国家具艺术作出令人赞佩尊敬的重大贡献。

Foreword

The earliest historical record of red sandalwood appeared on *Gu Jin Zhu* by Cui Bao of Jin Dynasty as a precious wood. *Li Dai Ming Hua Ji* by Zhang, Yanyuan of Tang Dynasty, described the fact that the ends of the scroll were made of Zitan in the imperial mansion because noted paintings would be incomparable if not. According to *Zhu Fan Ji* by Zhao, Rushi of Song Dynasty, Zitan was mentioned thereunder, and grew in Southeast Asian instead of China native soil. Imperial couches made of Zitan were found in the Yan Chun Ge in Dadu Municipality of Yuan Dynasty recorded in *Chuo Geng Lu* by Tao, Zongyi. *Ge Gu Yao Lun* by Wang Zuo of Ming Dynasty ranked Zitan as "rare and treasured wood".

Zitan is costly and rare because its producing area is remote where this rare wood grows extremely slow. Zitan utensils before Song and Yuan dynasties were hard to find except few pieces as checkerboards and mini-shelves still surviving in Japan's Seisouin Dome due to the transportation to Japan in Tang Dynasty. After middle period of Ming Dynasty China's southern territory was expanded and the ban on sea trade was lifted which results in a production of Zitan furniture in a small way. Pieces of zitan handed down from that time already become rare treasures.

The production of Zitan furniture became greater and greater in Qing Dynasty and is measured by scale till the time of Emperor Qianlong. Because Emperor Hongli, indulged himself with utensils displays, skillful craftsmen exhausted brains in search of bright idea to produce Zitan furniture, which lasted over dozens of years and prepared a considerable number of artworks, or "tribute make" Zitan pieces. Such furniture played a special role in the history.

Zitan furniture is the pride of China. Dr. Chan, Laiwa has deep understanding for Zitan culture, which compelled her to inherit and develop the traditional craftsmanship of it. She spent huge sum to purchase timber and employed well-known artisans to make Zitan furniture according to the specifications from the Palace Museum. She is so persevering that she even forgets herself thoroughly. For over years, she has pooled several hundreds of artisans and built dozens of workshops, which led to more than one thousand pieces of artworks. The scale and achievement can be described beyond the peak of perfection. In order to preserve such utensils appropriately and let them be viewed by people, and even for further reference and research, she built the museum on theme of furniture. Her action is historically and all the visitors could see how great contributions Dr. Chan, Laiwa has made to China, how she loves the civilization of China, and how she develops and promotes the Chinese furniture art.

郑欣淼
文化部副部长
故宫博物院院长

by Mr. Zheng Xinmiao
Vice Minister of Ministry of Culture of PRC
Director of the Palace Museum

序

在遍布全国、灿若群星的大小博物馆中，中国紫檀博物馆以其特有的魅力日益引人注目。

紫檀是极其珍贵的木材，紫檀家具是中华的瑰宝，紫檀艺术是中国传统工艺美术的精华，中国紫檀博物馆则是中国首家规模最大，集收藏研究、陈列展示紫檀艺术及鉴赏中国传统古典家具的专题类博物馆。由陈丽华女士创办的这一博物馆，虽然时间还不算长，但以其有别于传统的运行模式，颇多创新的展陈方式，注重与海内外同行交流的开阔思路，体现了生机与活力，成为中国民办博物馆的翘楚。

中国紫檀博物馆以保护历史遗产、弘扬民族传统文化为职志。明清两代是中国传统工艺的兴盛时期。明式家具是中国家具发展上的高峰，以其设计简练、结构合理、做工精巧、造型优美、风格典雅的特点，备受推崇和赞誉。清式家具，主要是清代康熙、雍正、乾隆三代出现的风格，总体来说是精巧华丽，由于运用各种新工艺，造成各种新式样，其中亦有精品，是明及以前所未见的。明清家具的工艺技术是宝贵的非物质文化遗产。陈丽华女士集中数百工匠，营建厂房，搜购良材，在专家的指导下，潜心制作明清式样的家具。人们从博物馆的精品陈列中，可以看到雕作技艺的高超。这些传统技术终于后继有人而不致湮没无闻，实为文化之大幸！当一批批参观者驻足紫檀宫时，当这些珍品在国外展出时，当一些精品被国内外著名博物馆收藏时，中外人士从中所体味到的是中华文明的独有情韵，感受到的是中华民族保护历史文化遗产的决心和努力。

从历史上看，作为工艺品的家具，既有实用功能，又有很高审美价值者，一般当首推宫廷家具。故宫是明清两代的皇宫，明代的“御用监”、清廷的“造办处”，都曾广蓄天下珍贵木材，汇集南北名师巧匠，专为宫廷制作家具。故宫博物院现收藏的明清家具，种类齐全，精品荟粹，在数量、质量及艺术性方面，国内外任何一家收藏机构都无可比拟。故宫还有一些著名的家具专家。这一优势，就使故宫博物院与中国紫檀博物馆结下不解的缘分。朱家溍先生等被陈丽华女士聘为顾问，指导他们的工作，并仿制故宫的一批家具，精心制作了一些故宫古建筑的微缩景观，如角楼、御花园中的千秋亭与万春亭等；宏伟的紫檀宫的修建，故宫的古建筑专家也曾悉心地予以指导。故宫为中国紫檀博物馆提供了多方面支持和帮助，紫檀博物馆则以自己的骄人成果使古老故宫的遗产得到复活，使这一中华传统文化得到传承。

中国紫檀博物馆能有今天兴旺的局面，当然与馆长陈丽华女士的努力分不开。她对传统文化、对紫檀艺术有热烈的追求，她不仅有着相当的鉴赏能力，同时又积极进行紫檀艺术的传承与创新。她投入巨额资金，花费大量心血，并自得其乐，坚持不懈。陈女士深知，企业的根基在社会，成功的企业应该回馈社会，报答人民。她不是把自己的珍藏及精美的制作当作待沽的奇货，或只是供个人赏玩的宝物，而要把它们公诸社会，期望更多的人能去欣赏，期望这一传统工艺得以永续流传。个人的爱好上升为一种文化的自觉，家具雕制的实践又产生出弘扬传统的历史责任感，于是就有了中国紫檀博物馆，企业也与文化结了缘。陈丽华馆长对博物馆始终充满着热情，在社会有关方面的支持下，正切切实实地推进着各项工作，使博物馆可持续地发展。

《丽质华堂》一书，让我们看到了中国紫檀博物馆的过去与今天；我们也相信，陈丽华馆长会以自己惯有的勤奋，继续书写未来辉煌的篇章。

2006 年 11 月

Preface

Just as there are many brilliantly shinning stars in the sky, so too there are many museums of different sizes spreading all over China. China Red Sandalwood Museum, with its unique charm, is becoming more and more noticeable. Red sandalwood is very precious. Furniture made from this wood is a national treasure. Red sandalwood art is the cream of Chinese traditional arts and crafts. The China Red Sandalwood Museum is the first and largest private theme museum in China. Specializing in the collection, display, and research of classical red sandalwood furniture and works of art, it fills a void in the field of Chinese galleries. The museum was founded by Madam Chan. Although it has not been in existence a long time, it shows great vigor and energy by using a non-traditional operating system and creative exhibiting techniques. It is a museum with broad ideas and a focus on communication with peers at home and abroad.

China Red Sandalwood Museum has assumed a mission to protect historical Chinese heritage and a duty to enhance traditional culture. Chinese traditional craft reached its culmination in the Ming and Qing Dynasties. Ming styled furniture also reached the zenith of its development. Artisans also created masterpieces in Qing Dynasty by using new craftsmanship techniques. The ability to craft furniture in Ming and Qing style is a precious cultural heritage. By seeking the directions of experts, gathering several hundred artisans together, building dozens of workshops and purchasing good timbers, Madam Chan has been able to replicate furniture of the Ming and Qing Dynasties. People are able to appreciate the superb carving skills as illustrated in the museum exhibits. It is indeed a blessing that those traditional carving skills have been passed to other generations and have not fallen into oblivion. Visitors coming to the Museum are able to appreciate the charm of Chinese civilization. They can sense the ambition of the Chinese nation to protect its historical cultural heritage. Similarly, when these masterpieces are exhibited abroad, or presented to other museums, people from foreign countries can have the same experience as those who are fortunate enough to visit the China Red Sandalwood Museum itself.

Historically, furniture which was both practical and artistic was normally reserved for imperial use. The Forbidden City served as the palace for emperors of the Ming and Qing Dynasties. Precious wood from all over China was stored in the "Imperial House" and at the "Manufacturing Department" in the Ming Dynasty. Well known artisans from both north and south China were gathered together to produce furniture for imperial use. In particular, lots of the furniture in Ming and Qing Dynasties collected by the Palace Museum is representative for use in the imperial households. In addition there are several furniture experts working in the Palace Museum. Because of a commonality of interest, the Palace Museum and the China Red Sandalwood Museum have forged an indissoluble bond with each other. Mr. Zhu Jianjin was employed by Madam Chan as her advisor to guide her work. Madam Chan reproduced much of the furniture collected by the Palace Museum and has also made architectural miniatures such as the Corner Tower, the Qian Qiu and the Wan Chun Pavilions in the Imperial Garden. Architects from the Palace Museum also directed, with utmost care, the construction of the grand China Red Sandalwood Museum. The Palace Museum supported and helped the China Red Sandalwood Museum in all aspects of its creation and development. Reciprocally and with great effort, the China Red Sandalwood Museum brought the ancient heritage of the Palace Museum back to life and facilitated the passing of Chinese culture to future generations.

The China Red Sandalwood Museum owes its flourishing prospects to the hard work of Madam Chan. She loves traditional culture and red sandalwood art. She is multi-talented, not only appreciating art, but also passing on and creating it so that it may be passed to future generations. She has spent sums of her money and spared no pain on red sandalwood art. At the same time, she was both persistent and content with here decisions. Madam Chan does not regard her delicate collections as rare commodities or solely personal treasures. Rather, she likes to share them with all of society. She wishes that many more people would have the opportunity to appreciate them and that furniture craftsmanship of the Ming and Qing Dynasties could be practiced by future generations. Her personal hobby has been transformed into a mission of making contributions to Chinese culture. The practice of making furniture has aroused in her a strong sense of historic responsibility to develop Chinese tradition. In this climate of national pride, an enterprise and a culture came together to give birth to the China Red Sandalwood Museum.

I can see the past and present of the China Red Sandalwood Museum from the book *Li Zhi Hua Tang*. I believe that curator Chan, through her customary assiduous work, shall continue to write glorious chapters for her future.

2006.11

文怀沙
中国国学大师

by Mr. Wen Huaisha
Master of Studies of Chinese culture

悠悠千古 器道合一

我中国古典家具，具高级美学特征，蕴华夏传统文化。形而下之为器，形而上之为道。器者，物也，厚德所载；为道，所涵盖至大无外。设器、道交融，浩浩乎穿越时空阻隔，岂不伟哉？天人共钦之奇观也。

古代家具至明、清两代，近乎器、道交融之佳例。其实用性与艺术性，邻书画、毗诗词，重在品与格，人性与神性之所寄焉。物与我、文与质、形与神、技与道、情与趣皆能高度和谐；方与圆、虚与实、直与曲、疏与密、轻与重诸多因素，由点、线、面有机结合，恍同凝固音乐。对称中求安稳、简洁中求静谧、空灵中求通透、变化中求秩序。余以一言以蔽之曰：“正、清、和”，儒、道、释精髓所尚也。

檀，佛家称栴檀（或作旃檀）木，梵名栴檀娜（candana），意为布施。见《佛说檀树经》、《正法念处经》等典籍，我国最早之诗歌总集《诗经》——《郑风·将仲子》、《魏风·伐檀》、《小雅·杜》诸篇，皆有檀之痕迹，足征其历史久远。紫檀亦称青龙木，旧有“寸檀寸金”之誉，昔为皇家贵族专用，寻常百姓难以问津。贤哉！吾友陈丽华博士，倾毕生精力与财力，精研檀木家具，并始建北京紫檀博物馆，斯馆巍然屹立于京郊。俾四方佳士接踵纷至，赏其体态、鉴其材质、品其光泽、味其韵致，由器入道，尽涤尘烦，顿消鄙吝，神往逍遥矣。

友侪为丽华女史作俚歌云：
丽华女史兮，逊清重臣之苗裔。中华革命大地初苏兮，门庭虽凋敝尚有余春；阶前器物兮，楠贵檀珍；十年浩劫兮，暴同沙尘；玉石俱焚兮，灭绝人伦；幸余一二兮，拆卸藏真；拨乱反正兮，正义重申；紫檀出土兮，复现金身；重加装合兮，檀宝更新。
丽华移居香港兮，海外经商；烟消雾散兮，大地重光。心系紫檀兮，梦绕家乡；承传国粹兮，仰望炎黄；广收残料兮，深入云贵、八下南洋；千难万阻兮，意志昂扬；三十春秋兮，成果辉煌；紫檀展示世界兮，耀誉遐方；歌林下高风兮，地久天长。

嗟乎！观赏历史，悠悠千古，器、道交融。鉴赏与收藏古典家具，非唯物质之需求，亦旨在慎终追远，修身养性也。

“周虽旧邦，其命维新。”丽华女史遴选紫檀馆馆藏，制成图片，结集付梓，以飨国内外之紫檀同好。弘扬国粹，泽古溉今之功不可没也。谨徇丽华女史雅命，草芜辞如上，颇自惭少文采、不足观，聊申敬忱云尔。

丙戌冬月公历二零零六年十二月十二日深夜
燕叟于云何孤寂斋

Matter And Consciousness Combining into One after Long years

Chinese classical furniture features elements of aesthetics and profound traditional Chinese culture. The furniture has both tangible and intangible components. It is called Qi (utensil) when referring to its tangible or concrete component. It is called Dao (consciousness or thought) when referring to its intangible or abstract component. Qi means substance. This virtuous character embraces all things on earth. Isn't it a spectacular event worth celebrating by both heaven and man, if Qi and Dao can be intermingled after they pass through the obstructions of time and space?

Furniture in Ming and Qing Dynasties serves as a best example of the blending of Qi and Dao. Similar to calligraphy and painting, the furniture's practical use and artistic quality are focused on taste and style. There is a harmony between the furniture and its user, between its shape and its soul, between its craftsmanship and its beauty. Many factors such as: square and round, practical and ornamental, curved and straight, loose and tight, light and heavy, are just as intrinsically combined as are the many musical notes in a symphony. It requires stability in the midst of symmetry, tranquility in the midst of simplicity, captivity in the midst of freedom, and constancy in the midst of change. They are Zheng (integrity), Qing (virtue) and He (courteousness) which is the core beliefs respectively advocated by Confuscius, Laozi and Sakyamuni.

The word Tan means almsgiving and is translated as "Sandalwood" in English. Tan has been recorded in various ancient codes and in records of Buddha's teachings. Also, it has been recorded in the book of Songs, China's first ancient poem collection. Thus, its remote past has been proven. Red Sandalwood is also called Qing Long wood. It is believed that one inch of red sandalwood is equivalent to one inch of gold. Red sandalwood had been exclusively reserved for imperial use and common people dared not make any proposals to even study it.

My good friend, Dr. Chan Laiwa, has devoted her energy and the fortunes of a lifetime to the research of red sandalwood furniture. She built the China Red Sandawood Museum which stands loftily in East Beijing. Continuous streams of visitors from at home and abroad come to China Red Sandalwood Museum. The texture, luster, and charm of the collections prompt the distillation of thought and purification of the mind.

I would like to take this opportunity to write a rustic song for Madam Chan:

Madam Chan is a descendant of a distinguished family of Nationality of Man in Qing dynasty. She still enjoyed the benefits of wealth and heritage handed downed from her ancestors even while her family was on the decline. Vessels and furnishings in her family were all made of precious red sandalwood or nanmu. The violent-storm-like ten turbulent years (a reference to the Cultural Revolution of 1966-1976) had disastrous consequences. Fortunately, a few antique pieces in her family survived this malicious destruction. She rescued the furniture by dismantling and burying the pieces until the end of Cultural Revolution in 1976, when once again she let the furniture see the light of day. The furniture remained intact and was even more splendid after the renovation.

After Madam Chan immigrated to Hong Kong, the substantial success of her overseas business ventures had not diminished her memories of red sandalwood and of her motherland. It is a responsibility of every descendant of Yandi and Huangdi to pass on the inheritance of the quintessence of Chinese culture. She collected timbers widely and eight times, visited India-Burma border and the provinces of Yunnan and Guizhou to obtain logs. She experienced innumerable dangers and hardships. However, her outstanding achievement of today is the result of her constancy of purpose for 30 years. She has shown the charm of red sandalwood to the world. She has made the Chinese red sandalwood art stand eternally like a tall and straight tree in the forest of art.

Now I feel all sorts of emotions surging up within me as I look back at the long process of history where after many long years, matter and consciousness have combined into one. The appreciation and collection of classical furniture are not only the pursuit of things material, but also the succession and development of culture.

Madam Chan, selected masterpieces from the collection in the China Red Sandalwood museum and compiled them into this book to facilitate their appreciation by red sandalwood lovers at home and overseas. She has rendered an outstanding service in the development of the best of Chinese culture. I was invited by Madam Chan to write an article for this book. I consider my literary talent unworthy of this honor, but nevertheless, I have written it to show my respect for Madam Chan.

11th Month of the lunar calendar, Bing Wu Year

At midnight Dec. 12th 2005

Written by Yan Sou at GuJi Study

陈丽华
全国政协港澳台侨委员会副主任
中国紫檀博物馆馆长

by Madam Chan Laiwa
Deputy Director of the Subcommittee for Hong Kong, Macao and Taiwan Compatriots and Overseas Chinese
Curator of China Red Sandalwood Museum

自序

我的祖上是满清八旗之一的正黄旗人，记得小时候，家里摆设的都是些祖上传下来的硬木家具，有架子床、顶竖柜、官帽椅、大画案，还有大插屏什么的。这些家具多是用紫檀、黄花梨木制作的，那典雅凝重的造型、寓意吉祥的图案，以及木材本身细腻的纹理和淡淡的清香，都让幼时的我沉迷。对于那时家里的摆设，父亲很看重，他常对我说，这些都是好东西，能攒起来就攒，不能攒起来就是挂在墙上摆着也好。也许就是从那时起，让我开始对紫檀产生了兴趣，并因此而成了我一生的追求。

算一算，从“文革”后期开始做古旧家具修缮，到回国开办紫檀艺术制造厂，再到今天的中国紫檀博物馆，我从事紫檀这项事业也应该有 40 年了。从不懂到精通，这期间的酸甜苦辣，只有我自己知道。紫檀作为木中的极品，产地偏远、成材极难，而且“十檀九空”，因而大料极其稀少。为了寻找紫檀，我八下印缅的深山老林，个中辛苦也绝非常人所能想像，但这一切也都过来了。现在想想，为了紫檀，一切的付出都值得。

这些年，做了那么多东西，迄今我没卖过一件，外人都很奇怪，觉得你光做不卖，那得耗费多少钱啊？我也这么想过，“寸檀寸金”啊，在紫檀上的投入，几乎是倾尽了我毕生的所有，我也想有回报。可是想想，还是不舍得。因为随着自己更深入地了解紫檀，我就越发清楚地认识到，紫檀艺术是民族的国粹，是中国传统艺术的珍品，把这些传统的文化艺术经由我的手恢复起来，把一批一批的工匠培养出来，让檀雕技艺能够从我这里传承下去，这才是我从事紫檀事业的最终目的。传统的檀雕艺术，讲究的就是手工制作，不用一根钉，榫卯插合，密不可分。不上漆，不上色，保持木材天然的纹理，这是现代工业不可能替代的。做一件，少则一年，多则得耗去数年的时间。这样的东西，卖一件就少一件，怎么舍得卖啊！当然，在以后的发展中，我也不排除通过拍卖等形式，让热爱紫檀艺术的中外人士拥有我的艺术品，毕竟艺术是没有国界的。

谈到我的紫檀制作和研究，就要说到故宫，说到单士元、王世襄、朱家溍这三位老前辈。可以说，他们是我的领路人，把我真正带进了"紫檀"这个大门。想想最初与三位老先生的认识，我迄今还记忆犹新。那是在1989年，我准备向北京亚运会组委会捐赠一件红木雕龙纹屏风，当时也是为了检验一下自己的水平，于是找了几位老专家做鉴定，其中就有这三位先生。开始的时候，他们都不相信我一个女人家能做出什么像样的东西来。记得这些老专家第一次走进我的雕刻厂时，我是又激动，又忐忑不安。我不知道这些老专家们能给我打多少分。直到看完我库房里的作品，单老紧紧握住我的手说"藏龙卧虎哇！"，看着其他几位老专家的笑脸，我一颗提着的心终于落地了。当又听说这些作品我一件没卖过时，老先生们更高兴了，当即就表示回去后向故宫博物院的院长汇报。于是从那时起，故宫便向我这个普通的中国女性敞开了大门。直到今天，故宫的院长换了一任又一任，但每一任的院长都给予了我极大的支持与关照，让我进到故宫的库房里临摹样子，丈量尺寸，还专门派宫廷部研究明清家具的胡德生先生长期在我的制作厂指导生产。在这之后的十数年里，单老还来过几趟，王世襄、朱家溍两位老先生也经常来看，指导我们的工作。他们对质量要求严格，在艺术上毫不含糊，对作品的尺寸一丝一毫的差错都不允许。所以说，如果没有三位老先生、没有故宫这么多年的支持，我是无论如何也不会有今天的成绩的。

在从事了多年的紫檀艺术制作之后，我渐渐感觉应该有一个场所，可以把这些东西展示出来，让更多喜欢紫檀的朋友来此观赏和交流。在萌生了这个想法后的1998年，我开始着手于中国紫檀博物馆的建设。在这个过程中，故宫博物院又一次向我伸出了援手。明式彩画老专家王仲杰先生、木作专家赵崇茂先生、瓦作专家朴学林先生，这些来自故宫的古建专家们，几乎是全天候地盯在现场，亲自督导各工艺的流程。所以，到博物馆来参观的客人，不仅被馆内精美的紫檀艺术品吸引着，也对博物馆本身古色古香的建筑赞叹不已。如今，中国紫檀博物馆已开馆近 14 年，接待了无数来自世界各地的朋友和各国的政要。近些年，我还携博物馆的藏品远赴美国、日本、韩国、马来西亚、台湾等国家和地区展出，在当地引起了极大的轰动。另外，为了更好地传播紫檀文化，让更多的人了解和认识中国的传统艺术，我又将馆内收藏的大型紫檀艺术品——“紫檀雕天坛祈谷坛·祈年殿”、“紫檀雕故宫角楼”、“紫檀雕万春亭”、“紫檀雕飞云楼”、“紫檀雕松柏交翠亭”等，赠送给包括中国故宫博物院、法国香博堡、美国史密森尼博物学院以及德累斯顿国家艺术收藏馆、日本九州国立博物馆在内的世界五大博物馆以作永久收藏。

说句实话，在从事紫檀事业的最初，我并没有想到会有今天这样的成就。从 1976 年到今天，将近四十年的时光，回首望望，这一路走来，充满着艰辛，也充满着无比的幸福，因为有紫檀一直陪在身边，有家人一直在身边默默地支持着自己。我的先生迟重瑞，是知名的表演艺术家，曾经饰演过电视连续剧《西游记》中的唐僧，却为了紫檀淡出了影视圈，多年来一直同我一起，勤勤恳恳，把全部的心血都融进了我们共同的紫檀事业之中。我的儿子赵勇、女儿赵莉、赵敏，对我十分孝顺，也非常支持我所从事的紫檀事业。我想，家人的理解和支持应该是我这一路走来最坚实的后盾了。

关于这本书，其实在很多年前，就有人劝我，该出本自己的书了，可我却以为自己还是个学生，迟迟没有付诸实施。直到 06 年，在诸位老前辈的鼓励下，在家人的劝说下，才有了《丽质华堂》这本书的面世。想想那一刻的心情，竟然又像回到了当年初识三位老先生的时候，兴奋，又不安，像个等待面试的学生。那期间，王世襄、文怀沙两位老先生对我的支持和教益让我备受鼓舞。两位老人，一个是研究明清家具的权威，一个是当代国学大师，当时都是九十多岁的高龄了，在听到我出书的消息后，他们在百忙之中放下自己手头的工作，为这本书出谋划策，并提供了许多极富价值的建议和忠告。王老为我的书题写了书名《丽质华堂》，即“珍贵的材质，华美的殿堂”，并在其撰写的前言里，称紫檀博物馆的建立“不云绝后，确是空前”。文老亲自撰文，对我在中国传统文化传承方面所做的贡献也极尽赞誉，令我受宠若惊，同时也深觉肩上的担子更重了。时任文化部副部长、故宫博物院院长的郑欣淼先生，不仅多年来对我的工作给予了大力的支持，还亲自为此书作序。借此，对于三位的鼎力支持深表谢意！

“可以说，这本书是对我从事紫檀事业几十年的一个总结，从第一次出版到今次修订再版，六年的时光转瞬即逝。回想一路走来，心中要感激的人实在太多，只有更好的传承发展紫檀文化才是对他们最好的感谢。

2011年9月，国务院公布了第三批国家级非物质文化遗产名录项目，中国紫檀博物馆申报的“紫檀雕刻”技艺榜上有名。2012年，中国紫檀博物馆又被北京市政府列为“北京市非物质文化遗产生产性保护示范基地”。两获殊荣，不仅体现了国家对传统手工艺的重视，也是对我几十载紫檀事业的肯定和认同。

悠悠紫檀，细腻婉雅，凝重华丽，绵远流长。我愿和所有热爱紫檀文化，热爱中国传统手工技艺的朋友们一起，通过我们的手，把先人留下的文化遗产一代代传下去，让中国的传统文化植根于我们每个人的心里，开花结果，绵延未来——

2012年3月

Author's Preface

My ancestors belonged to the Plain Yellow Banner, which was the most superior of the eight banners of nationality of Man in the Qing Dynasty. I still remember that in my childhood, my home was filled with antique hardwood furniture handed down from ancestors including a canopy bed, cabinets, yoke back armchairs, painting tables and a big screen. Most of the furniture was of red sandalwood or Huanghuali wood. I was captivated by their elegant and dignified design, the delicate texture and fragrance of the wood, and the implied auspicious meanings of the carved motifs. My father knew red sandalwood very well and he often told me that it is precious. We should re-assemble any broken red sandalwood pieces and if this was not possible, then we should display them by hanging them on a wall. Red sandalwood captured a place in my heart and became a major pursuit of my life.

My experience with red sandalwood spans thirty years. It started with repairing old furniture, to establishing a sandalwood art manufacturing factory, to finally building the China Red Sandalwood Museum. In that time I developed an intimate knowledge of red sandalwood. While red sandalwood is the best among all types of timber; it is extremely difficult to harvest logs of exceptional quality because 90% of mature red sandalwood trees are hollow. Due to encroaching populations, many of the remaining trees are in remote areas and large logs are rare. Eight times, I visited untraversed mountains and virgin forests in the vicinity of the India-Burma border to obtain logs. It is hard to imagine the untold hardships that I have experienced. I believe that the red sandalwood was worthy of the risks I took and the effort I expended.

I have made many red sandalwood furnishings and objects of art, but so far I have not sold a single one. People wonder how I could afford to continue making the pieces without recovering costs by selling some of them. Having invested all of my family fortune on red sandalwood, I had considered recouping some of my expenditures. The ancients so revered red sandalwood that they considered an inch of the wood to have the same value as an inch of gold. However, having thought about it more, I was reluctant to sell any of the pieces. As my study and appreciation of red sandalwood grew, I realized that this art form is one of the best examples of Chinese culture and tradition. Having come to this realization, my aims were to restore and preserve red sandalwood art and furniture. As well, I wanted a nice place not only to showcase these treasures, but also to educate more red sandalwood carving artisans. Traditional red sandalwood art requires a highly skilled craftsman. The furniture is made by using the tightly jointed structure of tenon and mortise. Not a single nail is used. The pieces are not lacquered or colored in order to maintain the nature texture of the wood. This construction cannot be duplicated by modern industry. It takes at least one year to finish a piece of furniture and sometimes it even takes several years. One forms a sentimental attachment to such pieces and so selling them is very difficult and heart-rending.

In talking about the study and manufacture of red sandalwood, I have to mention the Palace Museum and my three seniors: Mr. Shan Shiyuan, Wang Shixiang and Zhu Jiajin. They were my guides and led me to the red sandalwood world. My first meeting with these three gentlemen in 1989 still remains fresh in my memory. At that time, I was going to donate a red wood screen carved with dragon motifs to Beijing Asian Games Organizing Committee. It had taken years of meticulous care for me and my staff to design and make the screen. I had wanted my professional standard tested. I had invited the three senior experts from the Palace Museum to inspect the screen. At the very beginning, they did not trust me. They did not believe that a woman like me could create something of beauty. I remember that I was both excited and uneasy when the three gentlemen stepped into my carving factory. I was not sure how they would evaluate my work. As they began a tour of my furniture warehouse, Mr. Shan Shyiuan, tightly grasped my hand and whispered "We are in a den of crouching tigers and hidden dragons". The mention of these creatures made my heart leap since in China they represent things of high quality and good fortune. My fears vanished and a heavy burden left me when I saw the smiling faces of my guests. They were even more impressed by the fact that I had never sold a piece. They expressed their willingness to report my case to the director of the Palace Museum. Consequently, the door of the Palace Museum was opened to an ordinary Chinese woman. In the intervening years, the directors of the Palace Museum have changed several times. However, all of them have given me encouragement and support. They gave me permission to access their warehouses to copy designs and measure the size of the furniture. In particular, they sent Mr. Hu Desheng, researcher of furniture in Ming and Qing Dynasties of Palace Department of the Palace Museum. At my factory, he was able to supervise the manufacturing processes over a long period of time. Mr. Shan came to visit me several times after the initial trip to my factory. Mr. Wang Shixiang and Zhu Jiajin also visited often to direct our work. They were extremely strict on the quality of the artwork. They did not allow the slightest mistake and their expertise in art was beyond reproach. I owe my success and achievement in red sandalwood, to the generous help of these three seniors and the Palace Museum.

After many years work on red sandalwood art, I thought there should be a place to display them. This would facilitate viewing of the artwork by others who had an appreciation of red sandalwood. I was overcome by a keen desire to found the China Red Sandalwood Museum and in 1998 construction on this building started. The Palace Museum lent me a helping hand once again. Architects from the Palace Museum, Mr. Wang Zhongiie, an expert in the colored drawings of the Ming style, Mr. Zhao Chongmao, an expert in carpentry and Mr. Pu Xuelin, an expert in tiling, spent endless hours at the construction site, supervising various aspects of construction. Their dedication has ensured that visitors will not only be attracted by the delicate exhibits, but also by the grand design of the museum itself. The China Red Sandalwood museum has been open to the public for fourteen years. During this time it has received visits from countless tourists and important foreign political dignitaries. In the past two years the China Red Sandalwood Museum held exhibitions in countries and regions such as the USA, Japan, South Korea, Malaysia and Taiwan. These exhibitions were highly praised by people from all walks of life. In addition, to promote an appreciation for red sandalwood culture, and facilitate an understanding of Chinese traditional art by a greater number of people world wide, I made donations to the permanent collections of several museums. These donations consisted of large-scale red sandalwood models of ancient Chinese architecture as follows: the Temple of Heaven, the Corner Tower, the Pavilion with Six Corners, the Heavenly Pavilion and the Wan Chun Pavilion. The respective recipient museums included the Palace Museum, Kyushu National Museum in Japan, State Art Collections Dresden in Germany and Smithsonian Institute of USA.

To be frank, when I first became engaged in the red sandalwood undertaking, I never thought I would have realized the achievement of today. When I look back, nearly forty years has elapsed from 1976 to today. I have endured some extreme hardships, yet I have enjoyed the height of happiness on this journey because I was accompanied by beloved red sandalwood and supported by my family. My husband, Mr. Chi Chungsui, has been my tireless supporter in the cause of sandalwood art. My son Chiu Yung, and my daughters Chiu li, and Chiu Man, have been my source of strength and my family is the pillar and aegis of my journey in life.

Several years ago, someone suggested that I publish a book of my own. However, I procrastinated for several years. Until 2006, the publication of *Li Zhi Hua Tang* has become a reality. Thanks to the encouragement of my seniors and family. Now it is a time of mixed emotions for me, just as it was when I first met my three seniors. I was like a student awaiting an interview, my mood alternating between excitement and unease. During the time of preparing this manuscript, I was inspired by the support and instruction offered by two older gentlemen, Mr. Wang Shixiang and Mr. Wen Huaisha. Mr. Wang is an authority in studies of furniture in Ming and Qing Dynasties and Mr. Wen is a master of studies of ancient Chinese civilization. Both of them were in their nineties. After they heard about my book, they put aside their own work and offered me very valuable advice on this project. Mr. Wang also titled this book, *Li Zhi Hua Tang*, which means "Precious Wood and Magnificent Palace". He described the establishment of the China Red Sandalwood Museum with these words: "Though we can not say it will never happen again, it was at least never known before." I felt immensely flattered when Mr. Wen wrote a personal article highly praising my contributions to preserve traditional Chinese culture and my efforts to pass it on to future generations. Mr. Zheng Xinmiao, Then Vice Minister of Ministry of Culture of PRC and director of the Palace Museum has been a tireless supporter for many years and has personally written the preface for the book, too. I would like to take this opportunity to express my sincerest thanks to three distinguished gentlemen.

It could be concluded that this book is the summary of the career since I entered the course of red sandalwood. From the debut of this book to the revision and re-publication of it, six years has passed. Thinking back, there are so many people I would like to thank to, and the best way to express my gratitude is to continue inheriting and developing the culture of red sandalwood.

In September of 2011, the State Council published *The Third List of National Intangible Cultural Heritage,* and the technique of red sandalwood carving declared by China Red Sandalwood Museum is within. In the year of 2012, China Red Sandalwood Museum has been designated as the Productive Base of Protection and Demonstration of Intangible Cultural Heritage of Beijing by the Beijing Municipal Government. Through those two above, it could be drawn that not only the attention of the country is paid to the Chinese traditional handicrafts, but also it is a reflection of the approval of my career on red sandalwood for the past decades by both the Beijing and Chinese government.

As the red sandalwood carries an exquisite taste, its texture and form is neat, and it reflects a solemn, resplendent and profound culture, thus, I would like to take advantage of those hands that of those red sandalwood culture and Chinese traditional handicrafts lovers to pass on the cultural heritage from our ancestors to the upcoming generations, to instill the Chinese traditional culture in everyone of us, let it blossom and bear fruit in the future.

2012.3

中国紫檀博物館 简介

沿着长安街向东，在京通快速路高碑店出口的北侧，您会看到一大片的明清建筑群，这就是中国紫檀博物馆。它是由全国政协港澳台侨委员会副主任、富华国际集团主席、美国萨凡那艺术设计学院校董会董事陈丽华女士投资逾两亿元人民币兴建的，是北京市向建国50周年献礼的重点工程。中国紫檀博物馆是中国首家规模最大，集收藏研究、陈列展示紫檀艺术，鉴赏中国传统古典家具的专题类民办（私立）博物馆，填补了中国博物馆界的一项空白。

中国紫檀博物馆就其本身来说，就称得上是一件颇为完美壮观的工艺品。这座占地25000平方米的博物馆设计气势宏大而又处处精巧，古色古香而又不乏现代气息。仅正门就使用了400多立方米木材，并且全部是纯木结构，支撑大门的四根柱子高8米粗0.6米，无论是规模还是材质在北京的仿古建筑中都是罕见的。其五层主体建筑使用磨砖对缝工艺，毫米不差。1000多平方米的馆前广场，采用过去只有皇家使用的海漫斗板地面——大青砖铺设后再浸润桐油。陈丽华聘请来指导整个工程的，是建国初即在故宫博物院工作的木作专家、瓦作专家和画作专家，而这些专家一向被称作“活国宝”。

中国紫檀博物馆展厅面积9569平方米。设有中央大厅、陈列厅、会议厅、贵宾厅、多功能厅及临时展厅等，在这里您可以欣赏到：陈丽华馆长积数十年珍藏的明清家具陈列展示；有陈丽华馆长精心指导制作的传统家具精品展示；有佛教文化艺术品展示；有传统家具材料、造型、结构展示；雕刻工艺展示；另外在这里你还可以领略到微缩的中国古建筑景观：故宫的角楼，紫禁城御花园中的千秋亭与万春亭，尽显皇家气派；山西五台山龙泉寺牌坊，320条蛟龙姿态各异，精湛的圆雕、浮雕、透雕，世所罕见；古色古香的北京四合院，翘入云天的山西飞云楼……这些传递着东方情韵的艺术珍品，皆由珍贵的紫檀木演绎而成。

多年来，中国紫檀博物馆秉持着“继承、发展、创新”的经营理念，在传承与弘扬中国传统明清宫廷家具艺术和檀雕艺术上默默耕耘，并使之发扬光大。正是因为陈丽华馆长的远见卓识，使得濒临失传的紫檀雕刻工艺得到抢救、保护和创新。2011 年 9 月，中国紫檀博物馆申报的“紫檀雕刻技艺”被国务院列入第三批国家级非物质文化遗产名录。2012 年，又被北京市政府定位北京市非物质文化遗产生产性保护示范基地。

作为北京市一处重要的文化景观，中国紫檀博物馆于 2003 年底被评为国家 4A 级旅游景区，接待了来自世界各地的游人及各国政要，包括德国前总理赫尔穆特·科尔、国际残奥会主席克雷文先生及夫人、泰国公主诗琳通殿下、斯里兰卡议长恰马尔．拉贾帕克萨先生等都先后来中国紫檀博物馆参观并欣然提笔留言，对博物馆予以了极高的评价与赞赏。

为更好地在海外传播中国传统紫檀文化，中国紫檀博物馆先后在美国、日本、韩国、马来西亚、台湾等国家和地区的巡展，向世界介绍了中国，展示了中国传统的古典家具文化，受到了当地各界人士的推崇和认同。同时，中国紫檀博物馆还以另一种形式构架起东西方文化交流的桥梁，包括北京故宫博物院、德国德累斯顿国家艺术收藏馆、美国史密森博物学院、法国香波堡、日本九州国立博物馆在内的几家世界级博物馆都收藏有中国紫檀博物馆的作品。时任中国文化部副部长、故宫博物院院长郑鑫淼盛赞这一创举为中国传统文化走向世界做出了重要贡献。

未来，中国紫檀博物馆将继续以保护历史遗产、弘扬中华民族传统文化为己任。全方位高水平地展示紫檀艺术魅力再现中国传统家具的辉煌。

China Red Sandalwood Museum

Going east along the Chang'an Street, you will see a building complex to the north of the Gaobeidian exit of the Jingtong Expressway. That is the China Red Sandalwood Museum. It's owned by Ms. Chan Laiwa, who is Deputy Director of the Subcommittee for Hong Kong, Macao and Taiwan Compatriots and Overseas Chinese, chairperson of Fuwah International Group and a director of the Savannah College of Art and Design in the USA. The China Red Sandalwood Museum is the first and largest private theme museum in China with an investment of over 200 million RMB. It's a gift project for the 50th anniversary of the founding of the People's Republic of China and specializes in the collection, display and research of classical red sandalwood furniture and works of art, filling a void in the field of Chinese galleries.

The China Red Sandalwood Museum itself can be ranked as a grand and perfect artwork. With an area of 5000 square meters, the museum combines antique flavor and modern glamour. The whole design is magnificent with delicate inner parts at the same time. The entrance gate is of wood structure with more than 400 square meters of wood logs employed. The four supporting pillars are 8 meters high with a diameter of 0.6 meter. Both the size and the wood quality are rare in the buildings of traditional style in Beijing. The five-storey main building applies the technique of rubbed brickwork which makes the bricks fit together perfectly. The square in front of the museum is made of in tung oil soaked blue bricks, which were only used by the royal family in ancient times. The experts, who Ms. Chan has convened to direct the whole project are specialists in carpentry, tile and paintings and who worked in the Palace Museum after the founding of the PRC. These experts are honored in China and called "living national treasures".

The area of the exhibition halls of the China Red Sandalwood Museum measures 103,000 square feet (9569 sq. meters) and includes the central hall, exhibition hall, meeting room, honored guests' room, multi-functional hall, and temporary exhibition hall. On display are: Classical furniture of Ming and Qing Dynasties collected by Madam Chan for several decades, quality traditional furniture made by artisans under the supervision of Madam Chan, artworks of Buddhist culture and also raw logs and structure of the traditional furniture. Visitors can also appreciate models of well-known buildings of the old style. These include, the Corner Tower of the Forbidden City, the Pavilion of Ten Thousand Springs and the Pavilion of A Thousand Autumns. Both pavilions are located in the Imperial Garden of the Forbidden City. Also exhibited is a model of the Memorial Gateway at Longquan Temple of Wutai Mountain in Shanxi. This gateway is carved with 320 dragons in different postures. Other models include those of Beijing quadrangle dwellings and the Heavenly Pavilion in Shanxi. These artworks are made of red sandalwood and convey the eastern charm.

For the past years, aimed at the concept of *To Inherit, Develop and Innovate*, China Red Sandalwood has been inheriting and promoting Chinese traditional art of royal furniture in Ming and Qing Dynasty and red sandalwood caving. It is just because of the foresight and sagacity of curator Chan that saves the endangered red sandalwood carving technique and brings it further innovations. In September of 2011, the red sandalwood carving technique declared by China Red Sandalwood Museum has been included in *The Third List of Intangible Cultural Heritage* issued by the State Council; and in the year of 2012, China Red Sandalwood Museum has been designated as the Productive Base of Protection And Demonstration of Intangible Cultural Heritage of Beijing by Beijing Municipal Government.

As an important cultural scenic spot in Beijing, China Red Sandalwood Museum was awarded as the 4A National Grade Scenic Spot in the end of 2003, and has welcomed tourists and political VIPs all around the globe. Those political VIPs include, former Chancellor of Germany, Mr. Helmut Kohl, President of the International Paralympic Committee (IPC), Sir Philip Craven and his wife, Princess Maha Chakri Sirindhorn of Thailand and Speaker of the Parliament of Sri Lanka, Mr. Chamal Rajapaksa. After their visits, remarks have been left in pleasure, of which high appreciation and compliment is shown.

In order to better spread the Chinese traditional red sandalwood culture abroad, China Red Sandalwood Museum has successively made tour exhibitions in countries and regions such as the United States of America, Japan, South Korea, Malaysia and Taiwan, during which the culture of Chinese traditional furnitures was shown. Those exhibitions were highly praised and recognized by the local people of all circles. Meanwhile, China Red Sandalwood Museum built a bridge of eastern and western cultural exchange in another form, donating artworks made by China Red Sandalwood Museum to several world-class museums, such as The Palace Museum in Beijing, Dresden State Art Collections in Germany, The Smithsonian Institution in the United States, Château de Chambord in France, Kyushu National Museum in Japan and so on. Then Vice Minister of Culture of China, Director of The Palace Museum, Mr. Zheng Xinmiao highly appraised the innovative moves as a significant contribution to the course of spreading Chinese culture to the world.

In the future, China Red Sandalwood Museum will continue to take it as its own duty to protect the historical heritage, carry forward the Chinese traditional culture and exhibit the charm of red sandalwood in an all-round way and at a high level in order to re-present the glory of Chinese traditional furniture.

麗質華堂

王世襄題

中国紫檀博物館

乾清日照

中国紫檀博物馆
China Red
Sandalwood
Museum

克寬克仁皇建其有極

一　中国紫檀博物馆内景

——仿故宫乾清宫宝座间

An Interior View of China Red Sandalwood Museum

——Imitation of the Room of Throne from the Qian Qing Palace of the Palace Museum

二　仿乾清宫龙纹贴金大屏风

清式　原件藏故宫博物院

底座 440×65 厘米　通高 330 厘米

A Carved And Gilded Screen Decorated with Dragon Patterns

Qing Style　The original piece is in the collection of the Palace Museum

◎屏风参照故宫乾清宫陈设的金漆大屏风复制而成。屏分五扇，正中稍高，两侧递减，每扇顶端装屏帽，以透雕的云纹和龙纹为饰。屏风正中下部雕海水江崖图案，当中方框开光，内雕治国安邦的警言。屏座正面也仿照故宫的原物镶嵌各色宝石。

惟天聰明
惟聖時憲
惟臣欽若
惟民從乂
愷悌君子
四方爲則
首出庶物
萬國咸寧

三　仿乾清宫龙纹贴金宝座

清式　原件藏故宫博物院

长 130 厘米　宽 87 厘米　高 150 厘米

Imitation of Gilded Throne of The Qian Qing Palace

Qing Style　The original throne is in the collection of the Palace Museum

◎ 宝座参照故宫乾清宫金漆雕龙宝座复制而成，通体贴金。座面侧沿起边线浮雕火珠、朵云，四足作龙形，足下有须弥座。面上装围子，两侧各竖三根立柱，用底托和龙纹绦环板固定。后背四框镶成，板心正中圆形开光浮雕正龙。四角卷草蝙蝠，下部透雕夔龙寿字花牙。两侧立柱及后背顶端有九龙盘绕其间，龙身翻卷自然、雄劲有力。

四　紫檀雕龙纹大顶竖柜

清式　原件藏故宫博物院

长 218 厘米　宽 80.5 厘米　高 370 厘米

A Cabinet with Dragon Pattern

Red Sandalwood

Qing Style

◎紫檀木质。上箱下柜，均对开两门，以高浮雕手法雕刻云龙纹，苍劲有力，气势非凡。柜子四足包錾龙鎏金足，通体以紫檀木制成，用料考究尺量巨大，堪称紫檀家具之最。

五　紫檀雕博古纹大顶竖柜（一对）

清式　原件藏故宫博物院

长 218 厘米　宽 80.5 厘米　高 370 厘米

A Pair of Cabinets Carved with *Bogu* Pattern

Red Sandalwood

Qing Style

◎ 紫檀木制。其上下各开两门，中有活动插栓，下有柜肚，全部铲地浮雕博古图案，两柜纹饰各有不同。香炉、宝瓶、花卉等浑朴典雅　古趣溢于画外。柜两侧浮雕花卉纹饰。

六　乌木嵌金丝楠雕百子图大镜屏

清式　原件藏故宫博物院

底座 240×105 厘米　通高 340 厘米

A Mirror Screen Decorated with Inlaid Jinsinan Wood And Carved with The Pattern of *A Hundred Boys*

Ebony And Jinsinan Wood

Qing Style　The original piece is in the collection of the Palace Museum

---

◎ 屏框屏座均以乌木制成，正面镶大块玻璃镜，背面以金丝楠木制成，攒框镶心，四边有插销插入屏框。当中镶板心，浮雕百子婴戏图。雕刻技法高超，形象生动传神。

七　紫檀嵌玉雕五蝠捧寿大镜屏

清代　底座 345×35.5 厘米　通高 282 厘米

A Large Mirror Screen Decorated with The Pattern of *Five-Bat Supporting The Character Shou* (Longevity)
Red Sandalwood
Qing Dynasty

◎ 此镜屏系清代原件。以紫檀木为框架，采用传统手工技艺浮雕西蕃莲、云、海水、蝙蝠等纹饰，其底座雕西蕃莲，站牙雕云纹、海水纹、屏帽雕云纹和团寿字，并嵌倒飞的玉石蝙蝠五只，寓喻“福从天降”、“福寿齐天”，“五福捧寿”之意。雕工精细，线条流利，具有很高的观赏和收藏价值。

八　紫檀雕博古纹顶竖柜

清代　长 187.5 厘米　宽 72.5 厘米　高 320 厘米

A Cabinet Decorated with The *Bogu* Pattern
Red Sandalwood
Qing Dynasty

◎ 此柜格是清代遗留的原件。通体以紫檀木制成，其上下各开两门，四门镶板心，平雕斜万字锦纹地，又在锦纹地上高浮雕博古图案，香炉、宝瓶、花卉、宫灯等，浑朴典雅，古趣溢于画外。

黄花明月

中国紫檀博物馆
China Red
Sandalwood
Museum

九　中国紫檀博物馆内景

——明式正厅

An Interior View of China Red Sandalwood Museum

——The Main Hall in Ming Style

一〇　中国紫檀博物馆内景

——传统书房

An Interior View of China Red Sandalwood Museum

——Traditional Study

十一　中国紫檀博物馆内景

——黄花梨床、柜、案组合

An Interior View of The China Red Sandalwood Museum

——An Assortment of Furniture Consisting of A Bed，Cabinets And Tables Made of Huanghuali Wood

十二　黄花梨螭纹架子床

明代　长 226 厘米　宽 175 厘米　高 227 厘米

A Canopy Bed Decorated with The Chi Dragon Patterns Huanghuali Wood

Ming Dynasty

◎ 黄花梨木制成。床面下束腰，三弯腿，云纹足，牙板与腿镂出壶门，边缘起线。面上四角立柱，前沿加门柱，左右后及前沿两侧装门围子，以四合如意螭龙圆环攒接棂子板，木工术语称攒斗。床架上端四面装绦环板，透雕折枝花卉，四角夔龙纹倒挂牙子。此床为明代制品，原为藤编软屉，在床里的大边上还保留着穿屉的孔眼。明代黄花梨大器物存世极少，此物堪称珍品。

十三　黄花梨月洞门架子床

明式　原件藏故宫博物院

长 248 厘米　宽 187 厘米　高 240 厘米

A Canopy Bed with A Circular Entrance

Huanghuali Wood

Ming Style　The original piece is in the collection of the Palace Museum

◎ 通体黄花梨木制，四角立四柱，正面透雕四簇云纹加十字攒成棂子板，分三块，组成椭圆形月洞门。左右后三面均以同样手法装床围及眉板，浮雕暗八仙纹的倒挂牙子。

十四　黄花梨罗锅枨攒花架子床

明式　原件藏故宫博物院

长 225 厘米 宽 170 厘米 高 233 厘米

A Canopy Bed in Humpbacked Stretchers with Openwork Floral Patterns

Huanghuali Wood

Ming Style　The original piece is in the collection of the Palace Museum

◎ 通体黄花梨木制。床面立六柱，四面装床围，正面留出床门。上端装顶架，饰眉板，床围和眉板均透雕龙凤呈祥图案。面下有束腰，四面壶门牙条，三弯式腿，云纹足。

十五　黄花梨拐子纹席面罗汉床

明代　长 217 厘米 宽 126.5 厘米 高 84 厘米

An Arhat Bed (Couch) in Woven Top And Openwork
Rails of The *Guaizi* Pattern
Huanghuali Wood
Ming Style

◎ 此床为明代遗存原件，通体黄花梨木制。罗汉床又名“榻”，多设于客厅或书房。此床藤心床面，有束腰，壶门式直牙条。面上三面围子，用短材攒成透棂，造型上繁下简，相得益彰。

十六　黄花梨五屏风式镜台

明代　长 55.5 厘米 宽 36.5 厘米 高 72 厘米

A Five Panel Cosmetic Chest
Huanghuali Wood
Ming Dynasty

◎ 此镜台为明代遗存的原件，通体黄花梨木制成。台上四周有望柱栏杆，台座中安五扇面小屏风。屏分五扇，每扇由三块环板及亮脚构成。中扇最高，左右递减，并向前兜转。各扇搭脑均高挑出头，圆雕龙头，最上一块绦环板雕云龙纹。下为对开门式柜，装铜面叶、合页。屏风前是支架铜镜的地方，镜台雕刻甚为精细。

十七　黄花梨螭龙纹顶竖柜

明式　长 116 厘米 宽 54 厘米 高 218.5 厘米

A Cabinet Decorated with Chi Dragon Pattern
Huanghuali Wood
Ming Style

◎ 黄花梨木制。柜分两节，上下装柜门，以四簇云纹加螭纹攒成透棂。中间平设抽屉两个，在结构上起牢固作用。棂门攒斗繁而不乱，丰华典雅。木质纹理清晰美丽，具典型的明式家具风格。

十八　黄花梨团花亮格柜

明式　长 125 厘米　宽 55.5 厘米　高 195 厘米

A Cabinet Decorated with Tracery Floral Pattern
Huanghuali Wood
Ming Style

◎ 通体以黄花梨木制成。每扇柜门分上下两格，板心落堂踩鼓。上格方形绦环，内套圆光，浮雕牡丹双凤。下格绦环略呈长方形，浮雕牡丹双雀。柜下附几座，拱肩三弯腿，壶门牙浮雕卷草纹。柜内有格层，并安抽屉两具。

十九　黄花梨十字连方棂门柜格

明式　长 80.5 厘米 宽 42 厘米 高 141 厘米

A Cabinet with Cross Patterned Lattice Doors
Huanghuali Wood
Ming Style

◎ 黄花梨木制。上格三面透空，各装壸门券口。下部以小木料攒接成十字连方纹棂门，腿间亦装壸门式牙板。造型优美，纹理清晰，体现了明式家具文静典雅的艺术风貌。

二〇　黄花梨两屉攒花架格

明式　长 93 厘米　宽 41.5 厘米　高 167 厘米

A Two-Drawer Cabinet with An Openwork Floral Pattern
Huanghuali Wood
Ming Style

◎ 黄花梨木制。分上下两层，正中平设两抽屉，三面开敞，装壶门式券口。新奇之处在于极富装饰性的背板，采用几何纹透棂形式，工整严密，繁而不乱，与前部的简练形成强烈对比，有较强的艺术效果。

二一　黄花梨架格

明式　原件藏故宫博物院

长 100.5 厘米 宽 49.5 厘米 高 198 厘米

A Bookshelf

Huanghuali Wood

Ming Style　The original piece is in the collection of the Palace Museum

◎ 黄花梨木制，四框方材。共装屉板四层，中间夹抽屉。屉板四面透空，只在左右及后面装围栏。围栏以小木料作榫，攒成“品”字形棂纹，并在两面饰打洼线条，下层饰壸门牙板。为明式家具标准造型。

二二　黄花梨博古柜

清式　原件藏故宫博物院
长 109 厘米 宽 35 厘米 高 192 厘米

A Multi-Treasure Display Cabinet Carved with *Bogu* Pattern
Huanghuali Wood
Qing Style　The original piece is in the collection of the Palace Museum

◎ 黄花梨木制。分上下两部分，上部右侧和左下方作敞格，中间一格另设带束腰的小桌压在一角。下部右侧设抽屉两具，下格装两扇板门，浮雕花卉。左侧设亮格，高低错落，格下平设三个抽屉。设计新颖，典雅不俗。

二三　黄花梨雕梅兰竹菊亮格柜

清式　长 99 厘米 宽 39 厘米 高 181.5 厘米

A Cabinet Decorated with The Pattern of Plum, Orchid, Bamboo and Chrysanthemum
Huanghuali Wood
Qing Style

◎ 黄花梨木制。上格下柜，中间以抽屉分隔。上格三面透空，镶镂雕卷草圈口。下部对开两门，每门板心两镶回纹绦线，内饰梅、兰、竹、菊四季花卉，拐子纹下牙。造型典雅不俗。

二四　黄花梨多宝格（一对）

清式　长 70 厘米　宽 30 厘米　高 145 厘米

A Pair of Multi-Treasure Display Cabinets
Huanghuali Wood
Qing Style

◎ 黄花梨木制。架格开十孔，高低错落，四面透孔，前后两面均饰有透雕花牙。下部装抽屉三具，浮雕拐子纹，极具典雅清新之趣。

二五　黄花梨亮格柜

明式　长 81 厘米 宽 42 厘米 高 142.5 厘米

A Cabinet with An Open Upper Compartment
Huanghuali Wood
Ming Style

◎ 黄花梨木制。分上格下柜。上格部分背面镶板，左右及正面装透雕夔纹券口牙子。下设两门，落堂踩鼓镶板，壶门式牙板浮雕卷草纹，体现了明式家具的风格特点。

二六　黄花梨亮格柜

明式　长 113 厘米 宽 55 厘米 高 188 厘米

A Cabinet with An Open Upper Compartment
Huanghuali Wood
Ming Style

◎ 黄花梨木制。上格下柜。上格三面透空，各装壶门券口。下柜两门落堂踩鼓镶板，格柜之间镶板雕卷草纹。腿间装壶门式牙板，外翻足雕如意云头纹，寓吉祥如意。

二七　黄花梨雕龙纹联二橱

明式　长 160 厘米 宽 52 厘米 高 90 厘米

A Two-Drawer Coffer Carved with Dragon Pattern
Huanghuali Wood
Ming Style

◎ 黄花梨木制成，橱面有翘头。屉面贴券口，北京匠师称之为“灶火门”。券口下安带拉手的方形铜面叶，锁销可从券口之后的缝隙穿过，插及橱面大边底面的销眼内，此时锁销下端的圆筒与安在面叶上的两个锁鼻正好平列，如穿钉加锁，可将抽屉锁住。闷仓立墙雕龙戏珠。吊头下，前后都安挂牙，共四块，均有雕饰，在闷户橱中很少见。

二八　黄花梨小长桌

明式　长 112 厘米　宽 54.5 厘米　高 86.5 厘米

A Small Rectangular Table
Huanghuali Wood
Ming Style

◎ 黄花梨木制。凹线冰盘沿，四个圆柱腿直接支撑桌面，面下有极窄的牙条，两端牙头透雕卷云纹，牙下安圆料罗锅枨，造型简洁明快。

二九　黄花梨束腰展腿式半桌

明式　长 104.5 厘米 宽 64 厘米 高 87 厘米

A Rectangular Table with Splayed Legs and Waist
Huanghuali Wood
Ming Style

◎ 黄花梨木制。外形分为上下两部。上部宛如一具有束腰、方材、三弯腿外翻马蹄的大炕桌；下部则如无束腰家具的圆形腿足，其腿足看似如两段拼成，而实为一木连做。半桌束腰有波折，状如荷叶。正面牙条浮雕双凤朝阳、云朵映带，图案颇似明锦。侧面牙条雕折枝花鸟，有万历彩瓷的意趣。牙子下安螭纹托角牙，腿内装灵芝纹霸王枨。

三〇　黄花梨翘头案

明式　长 147 厘米　宽 46 厘米　高 82 厘米

A Long Table with Everted Flanges
Huanghuali Wood
Ming Style

◎ 黄花梨木制。案牙与腿夹头榫结构，案面两端翘头。圆柱腿，两侧腿间装双枨。通体光素无纹，简洁素雅。

三一　黄花梨雕拐子龙小书案

明式　原件藏故宫博物院

长 139 厘米　宽 75 厘米　高 85 厘米

A Small Writing Table Decorated with Guaizi Dragon Pattern

Huanghuali Wood

Ming Style　The original piece is in the collection of the Palace Museum

◎ 黄花梨木制。牙板浮雕拐子龙纹，两侧腿间镶圆材圈口，四角两卷相抵，足下不用托泥，而削出向外张出的撇脚。

三二　黄花梨裹腿枨长桌

明式　长 144 厘米 宽 84 厘米 高 88 厘米

A Long Table with Wrapped Leg Brace Ends
Huanghuali Wood
Ming Style

◎ 黄花梨木制。通体仨用圆材，线条圆润，牙条与枨之间装矮老，并镶炮仗洞拽开光绦环板，枨下安角牙。为了和枨相呼应，桌面边框立面用两层木材重叠而成，术语称为“垛边”。整体造型简洁明快，空灵秀雅。

三三　黄花梨雕拐子纹翘头案

清式　长 150 厘米　宽 38 厘米　高 85.5 厘米

A Long Table with Everted Flanges And Decorated with *Guaizi* Pattern
Huanghuali Wood
Qing Style

◎ 黄花梨木制。翘头，面下直牙条及牙头镂空拐子纹。两侧腿间镶方形圈口，边缘饰云纹，回纹方马蹄。

三四　黄花梨架几案

明式　长 312 厘米 宽 50.5 厘米 高 82.5 厘米

A Long Table with A Removable Top
Huanghuali Wood
Ming Style

◎ 此案由案板及几座两部分组成。两个几座为方形，四方腿，腿间装一具抽屉，足端刳成内翻马蹄，足下带托泥。通体光素面，整体巧妙运用黄花梨木质天然色泽和纹理之美，不事雕琢，天然成趣，榫卯结构极为精密，连接牢固，造型简洁明快。

三五　黄花梨圈椅（一对）

明式　原件现藏于故宫博物院
长 63 厘米　宽 50 厘米　高 98 厘米

A Pair of Horseshoe Armchair
Huanghuali Wood
Ming Style　The original piece is in the collection of the Palace Museum

◎ 黄花梨木制。仿照故宫收藏的紫檀圈椅制成。面下束腰，鼓腿彭牙，内翻马蹄，带托泥。面上四角立柱，背板正中透雕卷草纹。下端锼云纹亮角。两侧上下各装透雕卷草角牙。另在扶手尽头和四足两侧利用本来应剔去的木料透雕卷草纹，既美观又起到了加固作用。

三六　黄花梨方桌

明式　长 92 厘米 宽 92 厘米 高 84 厘米

A Square Table
Huanghuali Wood
Ming Style

◎ 黄花梨木制。圆腿直足，面下高拱罗锅枨紧贴桌面，枨子与四腿交接处采用裹腿式做法，在四腿内侧上部伸出霸王枨承接桌面。全器不施雕琢，尽显黄花梨纹理天然之美。

三七　黄花梨圈椅

明式　原件藏故宫博物院
长 63 厘米 宽 50 厘米 高 98 厘米

A Horseshoe Armchair
Huanghuali Wood
Ming Style　The origina piece is in the collection of the Palace Museum

◎ 黄花梨木制。面下有束腰，鼓腿澎牙，内翻马蹄，带托泥。面上四角立柱，背板正中透雕卷草纹。下端锼云纹亮角。两侧上下各装透雕卷草角牙。另在扶手尽头和四足两侧利用本来应剔去的木料透雕卷草纹，既美观又起到了加固作用。

三八　黄花梨交椅

明式　长 74 厘米　宽 66 厘米　高 107 厘米

A Folding Chair Deccrated with Ruyi And Cloud Pattern
Huanghuali Wood
Ming Style

◎ 黄花梨木制。绳面，交叉腿，腿下有托泥，并有脚踏。后背弧形，正中浮雕如意云头纹。椅圈等交接处用缠枝莲纹金属面叶包裹。工艺精美，极具代表性。

三九　黄花梨卷书式扶手椅

明式　长 68 厘米 宽 52 厘米 高 115.5 厘米

An Armchair of Scrolled Top
Huanghuli Wood
Ming Style

◎ 黄花梨木制。后背搭脑成卷书式，背板三段攒框打槽装板，分别饰以牡丹花纹、蝠磬纹及如意云纹，寓意福寿吉庆。扶手以委婉柔和的曲线与鹅头向上翻卷，后背板两侧下部及扶手与椅面下花牙由短木棂方条攒接成“拐子纹”，有子孙昌盛、安宁富贵之意。腿下端安管脚枨，自前向后逐渐升高，取其步步高升之意。

四〇　黄花梨玫瑰椅

明式　原件藏故宫博物院

长 59 厘米　宽 44.5 厘米　高 84.5 厘米

A Low-Back Armchair

Huanghuali Wood

Ming Style　The original piece is in the collection of the Palace Museum

◎ 此椅称玫瑰椅，黄花梨木制，这在明式的玫瑰椅中属于雕饰较为繁琐的一种。靠背板通体透雕六螭捧寿纹，横枨下安团螭纹卡子花。座面下三面券口牙子均有雕饰。

四一　黄花梨席心方杌

明式　长 48.5 厘米 宽 42 厘米 高 52 厘米

A Square Stool with Woven Top
Huanghuali Wood
Ming Style

◎ 黄花梨木制。座面席心，面下束腰，牙板及腿足里口起线。腿间装罗锅枨，足端内翻马蹄，体现了明式家具朴素大方的艺术风格。

紫云清風

中国紫檀博物馆
China Red
Sandalwood
Museum

四二　中国紫檀博物馆内景

——清式正厅

An Interior View of China Red Sandalwood Museum

——Main Hall in Qing Style

四三　中国紫檀博物馆内景

——传统喜房

An Interior View of China Red Sandalwood Museum

——Traditional Wedding Chamber

四四　中国紫檀博物馆内景

——传统卧房

An Interior View ɔf China Red Sandalwood Museum

——Traditional Bedrɔom

四五　中国紫檀博物馆内景

——紫檀嵌檀香双扶手屏风宝座间

An Interior View of China Red Sandalwood Museum

——The Room of Screen And Throne with Double Armrests, Red Sandalwood Inlaid with Sandalwood

四六　紫檀嵌檀香心花卉屏风

清式　原件藏故宫博物院

底座 370×60 厘米　通高 300 厘米

A Screen Decorated with Inlaid Sandalwood And Floral Patterns

Red Sandalwood And Sandalwood

Qing Style　The original piece is in the collection of the Palace Museum

◎ 紫檀木制。屏分五扇，上眉板和下裙板浮雕卷草纹，中间镶嵌以檀香木浮雕的各式花卉图，边缘饰紫檀雕云蝠纹，两侧及顶端饰透雕西洋莲屏帽及边牙。屏帽、屏身及底坐均活榫可开合。

四七　紫檀嵌檀香心花卉双扶宝座

清式　原件藏故宫博物院

长 155 厘米 宽 101 厘米 高 128.5 厘米

A Double Armrests Throne Decorated with Inlaid Sandalwood And Floral Patterns

Red Sandalwood And Sandalwood

Qing Style　The original piece is in the collection of the Palace Museum

◎ 紫檀木制。靠背、扶手及面下支架全部以清代流行的拐子纹攒接而成。在拐子纹的空当处又镶透雕夔凤纹的圈口花牙，同时均匀点缀檀香木雕刻的山水花卉图案。两扶手里侧又另加一道扶手，设计新颖。腿下带托座，附拐子纹脚踏。

四八　紫檀雕“山水人物图”屏风宝座

A Screen and Throne Set Carved with Images from The Painting *Figures And Landscape*
Red Sandalwood

四九　紫檀雕“山水人物图”屏风

清式　原件藏故宫博物院

底座 368×64 厘米　通高 300 厘米

A Screen Carved with Images from The Painting *Figures And Landscape*

Red Sandalwood

Qing Style　The original piece is in the collection of the Palace Museum

◎ 紫檀木制。屏分五扇，中扇最高，两侧依次递减。屏帽及两侧边牙透雕拐子龙（即夔龙），屏帽正中雕蝙蝠。屏框以四抹界出三格，上眉板浮雕蝠磬及卷草纹，中间屏心以厚料深雕山水人物图案。

五〇　紫檀雕“山水人物图”宝座

清式　原件藏故宫博物院

长 129 厘米 宽 80 厘米 高 119 厘米

A Throne Carved with Images from The Painting *Figures And Landscape*

Red Sandalwood

Qing Style　The original piece is in the collection of the Palace Museum

◎ 紫檀木制。座面侧沿及四周牙板浮雕水波纹，直腿回纹足，下承托泥。面上三面屏围，里框与板心之间镶檀香木雕刻的绳纹一圈，两扶手内外及背板浮雕山水风景。

五一　紫檀雕“海屋添筹图”屏风宝座

A Screen and Throne Set Decorated with Images from The Painting *Hai Wu Tian Chou* (Longevity)
Red Sandalwood

五二　紫檀雕“海屋添筹图”屏风

清式　原件藏故宫博物院

底座 300×60 厘米　通高 270 厘米

A Screen Decorated with Images from The Painting *Hai Wu Tian Chou* (Longevity)

Red Sandalwood

Qing Style　The original piece is in the collection of the Palace Museum

◎ 紫檀木制。回纹屏帽，屏心浮雕海屋添筹图。波涛汹涌的大海，海中有仙山楼阁，楼阁中陈设宝瓶，内插筹码，空中有飞翔的仙鹤，鹤口中衔筹码，欲往瓶内添筹。故事见于宋代苏轼的《东坡志林》。后来，在祝寿的礼物上常用“海屋添筹”图案来做装饰。

五三　乌木嵌紫檀雕“百骏图”插屏之一（总五件）

清式　座 196×70 厘米　高 176 厘米

A Slidable Screen of The Painting *One Hundred Horses*
Ebony Inlaid with Red Sandalwood
(First out of The Total Five Pieces)
Qing Style

◎ 五件成组，刻划清初西洋画家郎世宁的“百骏图”全景。屏座及屏框以乌木制成，浮雕西洋风格的卷草。屏心紫檀制，画面采用高浮雕兼镂雕手法，远山近水、树石花卉及百匹矫健的俊马，无不维妙维肖。画面雕刻章法有序，层次分明，显出强烈的立体感。

五四　乌木嵌紫檀雕“百骏图”插屏之二

A Slidable Screen of The Painting *One Hundred Horses*
Ebony Inlaid with Red Sandalwood
(Second out of The Total Five Pieces)
Qing Style

五五　紫檀雕“雍正抚琴图”插屏

清式　座 114×54.5 厘米　高 139 厘米

A Slidable Screen of The Painting *Emperor Yongzheng Playing the Zither*
Red Sandalwood
Qing Style

◎ 紫檀木制。屏框内四周镶透雕绦环板一圈，绦环板和站牙均透雕葫芦万代纹，正中板心浮雕雍正抚琴图。

五六　紫檀雕“天都溪流图”插屏

清式　座 139.5×79 厘米　高 234.5 厘米

A Slidable Screen of The Painting *Stream from The Heaven*
Red Sandalwood
Qing Style

◎ 紫檀木制。屏框饰混面双边线，里口打洼线，透雕蝙蝠葫芦纹站牙，蕃莲纹余腮板及披水牙，云纹墩子木，屏心高浮雕“天都溪流”图。

五七　紫檀雕月洞门架子床

明式　原件藏故宫博物院

长 246 厘米　宽 186 厘米　高 236 厘米

A Canopy Bed with A Circular Entrance

Red Sandalwood

Ming Style　The original piece is in the collection of the Palace Museum

◎ 紫檀木制。四角立四柱，正面以紫檀透雕四簇云纹加十字攒成棂子板，分三块组成椭圆形月洞门。左、右、后三面上下均以同样手法装床围及眉板，浮雕暗八仙纹的倒挂牙子。面上高束腰，装竹节形矮佬，浮雕花卉板心。托腮下壶门式牙条，深浮雕螭虎龙、灵芝及朵云。拱肩三弯腿，云纹式足。

五八　紫檀攒棂围子罗汉床

明式　长 206 厘米　宽 121 厘米　高 83 厘米

An Arhat Bed with Lattice Rails
Red Sandalwood
Ming Style

◎ 紫檀木制。三面围子，以短材攒棂，空灵飘逸。床身束腰，束腰下鼓腿澎牙，用料厚重，兜转有力，造型雅致，颇具文人风采。

五九　红木雕竹节纹嵌石罗汉床

清代　长 203 厘米　宽 112 厘米　高 105 厘米

An Arhat Bed Carved with Bamboo Pattern And Inlaid with Marble
Mahogany
Qing Dynasty

◎ 红木制。床架采用浮雕工艺通体雕竹节为饰。五屏式床围内皆镶石心，以镂雕松竹梅的花牙做迎手，四腿雕成竹根状，仿佛整个床就像几根竹子弯成的一样精巧。其设计新颖巧妙，雕刻圆润，既自然又古朴典雅。

六〇　紫檀透雕荷花罗汉床

清式　原件藏故宫博物院
长 220 厘米　宽 130 厘米　高 117 厘米

An Arhat Bed with Lotus Openwork Carving
Red Sandalwood
Qing Style　The original piece is in the collection of the Palace Museum

◎ 九屏风式床围透雕荷花莲蓬纹，面下束腰，鼓腿澎牙。束腰及牙条浮雕荷花莲蓬，腿、足处雕密不露地的荷花纹，内翻马蹄。

六一　紫檀雕云龙纹顶竖柜

清式　原件藏故宫博物院
长 115 厘米 宽 58 厘米 高 220 厘米

A Cabinet Carved with Cloud-Dragon Pattern
Red Sandalwood
Qing Style　The original piece is in the collection of the Palace Museum

◎ 紫檀木制。上箱下柜，各对开两门，以高浮雕手法雕刻海水纹、云纹及苍龙教子图。云纹流畅自如、龙纹苍劲有力。门下带柜肚，浮雕双龙戏珠，牙板正中垂洼堂肚，具清代乾隆时期风格特点。

六二　紫檀雕博古纹顶竖柜（一对）

清式　长 87 厘米　宽 35.5 厘米　高 187.5 厘米

A Pair of Cabinets Carved with *Bogu* Pattern
Red Sandalwood
Qing Style

◎ 紫檀木制。由柜和顶箱组成。上下各开两门，中有活动插栓，下有柜肚。正面五块面板高浮雕博古纹题材，既风格统一，又各自成趣，几案布置，瓶炉陈设，皆有出典依据。

六三　紫檀雕山水纹顶竖柜

清式　长 102 厘米　宽 51 厘米　高 208 厘米

A Cabinet Carved with Landscape Pattern
Red Sandalwood
Qing Style

◎ 紫檀木制。由柜和顶箱组成，俗称顶箱立柜。因大多成对，又称四件柜。其正面上下对开两门，中间装活动立栓，钉安錾花铜面叶及合页。柜架及门框里口起线，内镶板心，浮雕山水楼阁图案。云纹牙板，黄铜套足。

六四　紫檀雕仕女人物顶竖柜

清式　长 104 厘米　宽 52 厘米　高 209 厘米

A Cabinet Carved with Noble Beauties
Red Sandalwood
Qing Style

◎ 紫檀木制。由柜和顶箱组成，上下柜对开两门，中间装活动立栓，钉安錾花铜面叶及合页。柜门镶厚板，浮雕仕女图案，圆润生动，有很强的立体感。

六五　紫檀雕玉兰花顶竖柜

清式　长 102 厘米 宽 51 厘米 高 206 厘米

A Cabinet Carved with Orchid Patterns
Red Sandalwood
Qing Style

◎ 紫檀木制。柜门及柜堂板心均高浮雕玉兰花，寓意玉堂富贵。柜门四框饰混面单边线，活动立栓，錾花铜饰件，足下装铜套。系采用传统工艺作法，结构合理，布局严谨。

六六　紫檀雕荷花纹小立柜

清代　长 38.5 厘米 宽 19 厘米 高 71 厘米

A Small Cabinet Carved with Lotus Pattern
Red Sandalwood
Qing Dynasty

◎ 清代传世珍品，紫檀木制。形为顶箱立柜，实为一木连作。正面柜门及两山镶板框内回纹绦环，板心浮雕荷花，雕刻细腻。门下有柜肚，浮雕海水纹。柜身四框外角倒棱，足端装铜套，应为包镶作品。

六七　紫檀雕螭龙纹立柜

明式　长 100 厘米 宽 46 厘米 高 187.5 厘米

A Cabinet Carved with Chi Dragon Pattern
Red Sandalwood
Ming Style

◎ 紫檀木制。分上下两层，中间以抽屉相隔。上下各装两门，以四簇云纹及螭龙纹攒成透棂。下部两侧镶板，上部两侧亦镶透棂，富于变化。

六八　紫檀嵌螺钿千字文立柜

清式　长 117 厘米 宽 57.5 厘米 高 206 厘米

A Cabinet with Inlaid *One-Thousand-Word Essay* of Mother-of-Pearl

Red Sandalwood

Qing Style

◎ 紫檀木制。柜分两层，上层较高，下层较短。柜的两侧面浮雕拐子纹，正面上下各开两门，柜门上采用螺钿镶嵌工艺，以行书体嵌南北朝周兴嗣所作《千字文》全文。

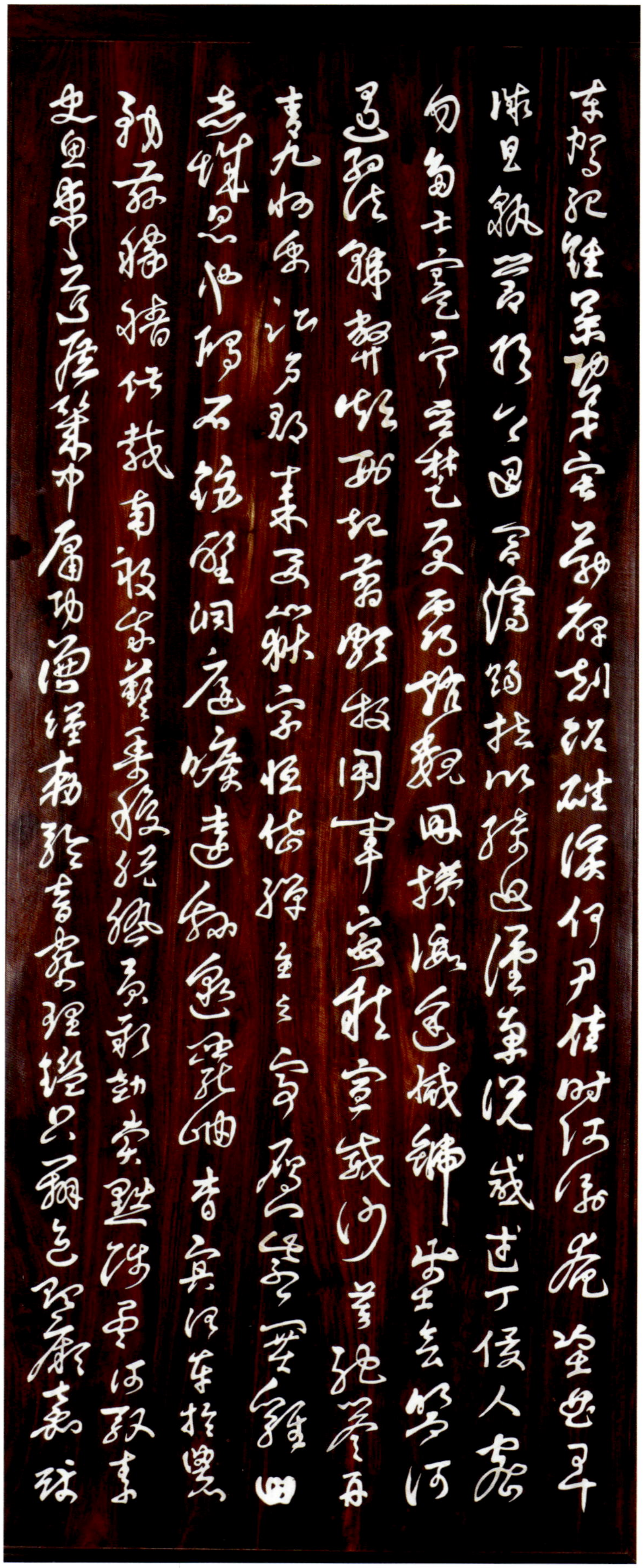

六九　紫檀棂门柜格

明式　长 106.5 厘米　宽 51 厘米　高 187 厘米

A Cabinet with Lattice Doors
Red Sandalwood
Ming Style

◎ 紫檀木制。上分三层，下有几座。后装背板，正面木轴直棂门两扇。直棂分三段，中以两道扁方框作隔，侧面透棂做法相同。几座设抽屉两具，下有屉板，中部留有空间，屉板下安素牙头。

七〇　紫檀灯笼锦柜格

明式　长 108 厘米 宽 39 厘米 高 185 厘米

A Shelving Cabinet with Lantern Shape Lattice Doors
Red Sandalwood
Ming Style

◎ 紫檀木制。格分四层，四面透空，只在中间对开两门，用短材攒成灯笼锦纹，棱角打磨圆润，不加雕饰，突出了朴素典雅的艺术特点。

七一　紫檀十字连方绳纹柜格

明式　长 91 厘米 宽 44 厘米 高 202 厘米

A Shelving Cabinet with Cord Patterned Lattice Doors
Red Sandalwood
Ming Style

◎ 紫檀木制。上格下柜，中设抽屉两具。上格两层，三面透空。下边设围竺，栏下矮佬界分，镶檀香木透雕绳纹绦环。屉下对开两门，以十字连方形式攒接成几何棂纹。

七二　紫檀博古柜格

清式　长 87 厘米 宽 35.5 厘米 高 187.5 厘米

A Multi-Treasure Display Cabinet Carved with *Bogu* Pattern
Red Sandalwood
Qing Style

◎ 紫檀木制。上格下柜，间隔抽屉。上格开敞，以陈器玩。下部对开两门，绦环内浮雕博古纹。黄铜面叶拉手，具有意想不到的装饰作用。

七三　紫檀多宝格

清式　长 106 厘米 宽 30 厘米 高 171 厘米

A Multi-Treasure Display Cabinet
Red Sandalwood
Qing Style

◎ 紫檀木制。多宝格一般成对陈设，左右对称。格分八层，高低错落，分出大小不同的空间，用以陈设各种摆件。架格四面透空，可以从不同方向观赏陈设品。

七四　紫檀嵌五色玻璃雕龙凤纹多宝格

清式　原件藏上海博物馆

长 179 厘米　宽 81.5 厘米　高 228 厘米

A Multi-Treasure Display Cabinet with Dragon-Phoenix Pattern And Multi-Color Glass Inlaid

Red Sandalwood

Qing Style　The original piece is in the collection of the Shanghai Museum

◎ 紫檀木制。正面帽顶下圆雕凤纹，弯腿彭出幅度较大，并以兰花为饰。格门以五色压花玻璃制成，代表五色国土，与柜角的金属包角一起有江山稳固牢不可破的寓意。柜身通体雕刻龙纹、竹节纹及鱼鸟纹等传统吉祥图案。另刻有 60 只形态各异的仙鹤，据传是当年慈禧寿辰时臣子们所送的贺礼。

七五　紫檀梳妆台

清式　长 120 厘米　宽 61.5 厘米　高 198 厘米

A Dressing Table
Red Sandalwood
Qing Style

◎ 紫檀木制。造型仿清代晚期流行的式样。台面以下设抽屉两排分列左右，三弯形鹰爪足。台面中间向内凹，面上装玻璃镜，两侧饰雕花窗格，镜侧有小平台及抽屉。整体造型雍容华贵。

七六　紫檀雕绳纹拱璧小长桌

清式　原件藏故宫博物院

长 100.5 厘米　宽 36 厘米　高 83 厘米

A Small Long Table Decorated with Cord Pattern And *Bi* (A Round Flat Piece of Jade with A Hole in The Center)

Red Sandalwood

Qing Style　The original piece is in the collection of the Palace Museum

◎ 紫檀木制。面下束腰，镂雕炮仗洞，下衬托腮，牙下以绳纹拱璧的装饰手法取代了罗锅枨及矮佬。

七七 紫檀雕树石人物联三橱

清式 长 188 厘米 宽 45 厘米 高 90.5 厘米

A Three-Drawer Coffer Carved with Figures And Landscape
Red Sandalwood
Qing Style

◎ 紫檀木制。案形平头，面下平装抽屉三具，绦环板内浮雕松树人物图。再下装柜门四扇，可启闭。柜下装牙条。两腿外侧装托角牙板 浮雕树石人物图。在抽屉面和柜门上装錾花黄铜饰件，可以上锁。整体美观大方，做工精细，具清代中期风格。

七八　紫檀雕云龙纹漆面长桌

清代　长 165 厘米 宽 69 厘米 高 90 厘米

A Lacquered Long Table with Cloud-Dragon Pattern
Red Sandalwood
Qing Dynasty

◎ 此桌为清代原件。素漆桌面，除桌面外，通体以紫檀雕云龙纹为骨架，共雕九十九条形态各异、大小不同的龙。其雕刻手法精细，气韵生动，富有动感，桌子的四角及四足均包有刻着云龙图案的铜包角，为清代皇家御用之作。

七九　紫檀雕海水纹束腰几形画案

明式　原件藏故宫博物院

长 172 厘米 宽 75 厘米 高 84 厘米

A Painting Table with Waist And Sea-Waving Pattern

Red Sandalwood

Ming Style　The orig.nal piece is in the collection of the Palace Museum

◎ 紫檀木制。造型仿炕几，鼓腿澎牙，新奇之处在于四腿不是向四角方向，而是向两侧鼓出。除案面外，通体雕刻海水纹。另在腿下的托泥正中又上翻海水纹。

八〇　紫檀雕缠枝莲带托泥平头案

清式　原件藏故宫博物院

长 258 厘米　宽 51 厘米　高 90 厘米

A Flat Long Table with Base Stretchers And Intertwined Lotus Flower Pattern

Red Sandalwood

Qing Style　The original piece is in the collection of the Palace Museum

---

◎ 紫檀木制。面下牙板镂雕成如意纹云头，牙头与腿部用挂肩榫结合，腿间装透雕档板，下垫须弥式托泥座。

八一　紫檀雕鱼门洞回纹足平头案

清式　长 170 厘米 宽 44.5 厘米 高 90 厘米

A Flat Table with Openwork Waist And Key-Fret Patterned Legs
Red Sandalwood
Qing Style

◎ 紫檀木制。面下镶板锼出鱼门洞，两侧回纹卷头。面下两个灯笼双翻回纹几座，中间以透雕卷草花连接，共同承托案面。

八二　紫檀雕八仙人物方桌

清式　长 92 厘米　宽 92 厘米　高 84.5 厘米

A Square Table Decorated with The Eight Immortals
Red Sandalwood
Qing Style

◎ 紫檀木制。四面牙板下饰透雕八仙人物花牙，面下直束腰，直腿回纹马蹄足。八仙纹大多只雕出八仙手持之物，俗称暗八仙，此桌以人物形象表现，极为少见，弥足珍贵。

八三　紫檀雕云蝠纹展腿方桌

清式　长 87.5 厘米　宽 87.5 厘米　高 84 厘米

A Square Table with Splayed Legs And Cloud-Bat Pattern

Red Sandalwood

Qing Style

◎ 紫檀木制。面下打洼束腰，拱肩展腿外翻马蹄。牙板及四腿上皆浮雕云蝠纹。

八四　紫檀嵌黄杨木琴桌

清式　长 92 厘米 宽 34 厘米 高 90.5 厘米

A Zither Table Inlaid with Boxwood
Red Sandalwood And Boxwood
Qing Style

◎ 紫檀木制。两端书卷式。面下有黄杨木雕拐子纹花牙。并有横枨连接，两卷头及腿间镶透雕螭纹绦环板。四腿下拐子纹外翻足，横枨上镶透雕拐子纹圈口。琴桌前脸另装档板，框内以四簇云纹攒成大面积棂子板，既增加了牢固性，又收到很好的装饰效果。

八五　紫檀拐子纹卷头案

清式　长 125 厘米　宽 40 厘米　高 81 厘米

A Long Table with Scrolled Ends And *Guaizi* Pattern
Red Sandalwood
Qing Style

◎ 紫檀木制。两头下卷成水波纹，面下装拐子纹花牙，直腿方马蹄，腿间装横枨。

八六　紫檀嵌瘿木梅花式圆桌

清式　直径 98 厘米 高 82 厘米

A Plum Blossom Shaped Table with Burlwood Inlaid on Top
Red Sandalwood
Qing Style

◎ 紫檀木制。桌面梅花形，镶瘿木心，面下随形饰透雕梅花。五条腿作曲线形，内装霸王枨。腿面浮雕梅花纹，五腿间装冰裂纹圆底，既起装饰作用，又加固腿足。

八七　紫檀雕缠枝牡丹半圆桌

清式　半径 52.5 厘米 高 79.5 厘米

A Semi-Circular Table with Intertwined Peony Pattern
Red Sandalwood
Qing Style

◎ 紫檀木制。半圆形，镶瘿木心，面下有束腰。腿及牙条以报肩榫相接，四腿间上部安透雕卷草缠枝牡丹花牙，下部安四根随形平行枨装透雕缠枝牡丹花纹半圆底屉，既起装饰作用，又加固腿足，有四平八稳之意。

八八　紫檀嵌瘿木方几

清式　长 44 厘米 宽 44 厘米 高 80.5 厘米

A Square Censer Table Decorated with Burlwood Inlaid Red Sandalwood

Qing Style

◎ 紫檀木制。几面上嵌黄花梨瘿木。面下高束腰，四周各镶浮雕凤纹花板，牙板正中垂洼堂肚，浮雕山水人物。直腿回纹足，四面平管脚枨。

八九　紫檀石面双层小几

清式　长 32 厘米 宽 17.5 厘米 高 27.5 厘米

A Stool with Combined Two-Layer Design And Marble Top Inlaid
Red Sandalwood
Qing Style

◎ 紫檀木制。几腿为展腿式，抱间榫结构。有束腰，上卷式外翻云纹足，牙板洼堂肚，下部装罗锅枨。下层面镶方形大理石心，上层面镶圆形大理石心。通体光素，造型简练。

九〇　紫檀四出头官帽椅

明式　座面 58.5 × 47 厘米　通高 119.5 厘米

A *Sichutou Guanmaoyi* (A Yoke Back Armchair Which Resembles An Ancient Northern Chinese Official Hat)
Red Sandalwood
Ming Style

◎ 紫檀木制。后柱、搭脑、扶手、鹅脖及联帮棍均施以委婉柔和的曲线，造型优美。面下正面装壶门式券口，腿间“步步高”赶枨，侧脚收分明显可见。

九一　紫檀席面南官帽椅

明式　长 75 厘米 宽 59 厘米 高 110 厘米

A *Nan Guanmaoyi* (A Yoke Back Armchair Which Resembles An Ancient Southern Chinese Official Hat) with Cushion
Red Sandalwood
Ming Style

◎紫檀木制。座面镶席心，前宽后窄呈扇面式，面下鱼肚形牙板，圆腿直足，腿间安“步步高”赶枨，寓意步步高升。另其搭脑左右和扶手前端均不出挑，且貌似古代南方官员的帽子，因而得名“南官帽椅”。

九二　紫檀雕蝠寿纹扶手椅

清式　原件藏故宫博物院

座面 62.5 × 50 厘米　通高 104.5 厘米

An Armchair Decorated with Bats And The Chinese Character *Shou* (Longevity)

Red Sandalwood

Qing Style　The original piece is in the collection of the Palace Museum

◎ 紫檀木制。椅背、扶手以拐子纹攒成，靠背板浮雕蝙蝠及圆寿字，下饰两夔龙。面下束腰，牙下正中雕如意纹洼堂肚，直腿回纹足，四面平管脚枨。

九三　紫檀嵌檀香心扶手椅

清式　原件藏故宫博物院

座面 66×51 厘米　通高 108 厘米

An Armchair with Sandalwood Inlaid Red Sandalwood And Sandalwood

Qing Style　The orig nal piece is in the collection of the Palace Museum

◎ 紫檀木制。后背搭脑与立柱云纹交接，扶手及靠背板浮雕拐子纹，背板镶嵌檀香木雕的蝙蝠纹。面下束腰，四面馊拐子纹花牙，四面平底枨。

九四　紫檀雕西洋花扶手椅

清式　原件藏故宫博物院

座面 64.5 × 52 厘米　通高 114.5 厘米

An Armchair Decorated with Western Grass
Red Sandalwood

Qing Style　The original piece is in the collection of the Palace Museum

◎ 紫檀木制。座面落堂踩鼓，面下仰莲上托腮，澎牙三弯腿，浮雕西洋卷草纹。鹰爪式四足，带托泥。面上后背及扶手取西洋巴洛克式样，搭脑雕饰螺壳，背板及框架内均饰以西洋卷草。

九五　紫檀雕西番莲扶手椅

清式　原件藏故宫博物院

座面 66×51 厘米　通高 111 厘米

An Armchair Deccrated with Passion Flowers

Red Sandalwood

Qing Style　The original piece is in the collection of the Palace Museum

---

◎ 紫檀木制。椅背搭脑上拱，背板略带曲弯，浮雕西番莲。后背与背边柱内口及扶手内口均透雕西洋卷草。面下束腰，卷草纹，洼堂肚及托端角花，四面平底枨。

九六　紫檀雕缠枝莲扶手椅

清式　原件藏故宫博物院
座面 64×52 厘米　通高 115 厘米

An Armchair Decorated with Intertwined Lotus
Red Sandalwood
Qing Style　The original piece is in the collection of the Palace Museum

◎ 紫檀木制，清代广式风格。椅背、搭脑用大料镂雕成云纹，空当处留料雕刻成厚一厘米的西式卷草，靠背板亦以云纹饰边，正中浮雕磬纹及西番莲，扶手镂雕云纹，与搭脑融为一体。面下束腰，四面平底枨，牙板下四面镶回纹券口，枨下四面洼堂肚牙条。

九七　紫檀雕山水人物扶手椅

清式　座面 70×52 厘米　通高 98 厘米

An Armchair Deccrated with Landscape And Figures
Red Sandalwood
Qing Style

◎ 紫檀木制。椅背、搭脑及扶手圆雕草龙纹，椅背及扶手框内镶板，浮雕山水人物及树石楼台，雕刻手法圆润柔和。面下高束腰，衬莲瓣托腮，牙板及腿足上截浮雕卷草纹，足下罗锅式托泥。

九八　紫檀雕八仙过海人物扶手椅

清式　长 69.5 厘米 宽 50 厘米 高 102 厘米

An Armchair Decorated with The Eight Immortals
Red Sandalwood
Qing Style

◎ 紫檀木制。此椅造型仿清代晚期风格，搭脑及扶手高雕蝠云纹及海水江崖图案，椅背及扶手框内镶板，浮雕八仙人物、树石楼阁及暗八仙图案。雕刻手法圆润柔和，面下高束腰饰卷草纹，牙条浮雕寿桃硕果间饰缠枝卷草纹，四足端雕回纹，足下带托泥。

九九　紫檀雕梅花绣墩

清式　面径 31.5 厘米　高 51 厘米

A Drum Stool Decorated with Plum Blossoms
Red Sandalwood
Qing Style

◎ 紫檀木制。五瓣梅花式，面下束腰。束腰下饰托腮，鼓腿澎牙，坐落在梅花式托泥上。腿间饰开光洞，镂雕梅花。梅开五瓣，象征五福。

一〇〇　紫檀五开光绣墩

清式　原件藏故宫博物院
面径 37.5 厘米　高 50 厘米

A Drum Stool with Five Side Openings
Red Sandalwood
Qing Style　The original piece is in the collection of the Palace Museum

◎ 紫檀木制。造型特点仿花鼓，上下各雕一道象征固定鼓皮的弦纹及乳钉。中间弧形腹腔，浮雕卷云纹。五足之间锼出曲边开光亮洞。设计巧妙，稳重大方。

金絲絕唱

中国紫檀博物馆
China Red
Sandalwood
Museum

一〇一　中国紫檀博物馆内景

——贵宾接待室

An Interior View of China Red Sandalwood Museum

——Reception Room for Honorable Guests

一〇二　中国紫檀博物馆内景
—— 金丝楠雕葫芦万代落地花罩

An Interior View of China Red Sandalwood Museum
——A Floral Patterned Archway of Jinsinan Wood

一〇三　金丝楠雕“山水楼阁图”屏风宝座

清式　原件藏故宫博物院

A Screen and Throne Set Carved with Images from The Painting *Landscape*
Jinsinan Wood
Qing Style　The original piece is in the collection of the Palace Museum

一〇四　金丝楠雕“山水楼阁图”屏风

清式　原件藏故宫博物院

底座 238×44 厘米　通高 213 厘米

A Screen Carved with Images from The Painting *Landscape*

Jinsinan Wood

Qing Style　The original piece is in the collection of the Palace Museum

◎ 用明代遗存的金丝楠木制成。回纹打洼边，屏心以高浮雕手法雕刻山水楼阁、人物、树石、花卉等。图案雕刻刀法圆润，一丝不苟。屏下承直形屏座，两端前后各出纵向垛头，以三支站牙抵夹。

一〇五　金丝楠雕灵芝插屏

清式　原件藏故宫博物院

座 95.5×50 厘米　通高 111 厘米

A Slidable Screen with *Lingzhi* (Ganoderma Lucidum Karst) Carving

Jinsinan Wood

Qing Style　The original piece is in the collection of the Palace Museum

◎ 用明代遗存的金丝楠木制成。式样仿照故宫所藏的大灵芝插屏。屏框与底座立柱一木连作，余腮板浮雕卷云纹。回纹洼堂肚、披水牙。屏心正中雕灵芝，背面以隶书阴刻清代乾隆皇帝的灵芝诗。

一〇六　金丝楠雕云龙纹顶竖柜（一对）

清式　原件藏故宫博物院

长 115 厘米　宽 58 厘米　高 220.5 厘米

A Pair of Cabinets Carved with Cloud-Dragon Pattern
Jinsinan Wood
Qing Style

◎ 此柜用明代遗存的金丝楠木制成，系仿照故宫乾清宫陈设的紫檀大柜制作。上箱下柜，各对开两门，以高浮雕手法雕刻海水纹、云纹及苍龙教子图。云纹流畅自如，龙纹苍劲有力。门下带柜肚，浮雕双龙戏珠，牙板正中垂洼堂肚。具清代乾隆时期风格特点。

一〇七　金丝楠雕葫芦纹方桌

清式　长 100 厘米 宽 100 厘米　高 86 厘米

A Square Table Decorated with Calabash Patterns
Jinsinan Wood
Qing Style

◎ 以明代遗存的金丝楠木制成。面下带束腰，腿间装曲边透雕牙板，牙头稍低 既加固了四足，又有很好的装饰作用。

一〇八　金丝楠雕葫芦纹扶手椅（一对）

清式　原件藏故宫博物院

长 63 厘米　宽 51 厘米　高 96 厘米

A Pair of Armchairs Decorated with Calabash Patterns Jinsinan Wood

Qing Style　The original piece is in the collection of the Palace Museum

◎ 以金丝楠木制成，系明代遗存旧料，十分珍贵。椅子造型采用清代晚期风格，椅背及扶手以透雕手法饰葫芦及如意纹，寓意子孙万代。

一〇九　金丝楠架几案

清式　原件藏故宫博物院
长 366.5 厘米 宽 56.5 厘米 高 105 厘米

A Long Table with A Removable Top
Jinsinan Wood
Qing Style

◎ 以明代遗存的金丝楠木制成。案面用整块木料，面下几腿中间装屉板，下装雪脚枨。案侧面浮雕八宝纹，俗谓“八吉祥”。几腿上空饰透雕葫芦纹券口，下空装壶门式圈口，浮雕卷草纹。用料粗硕，稳重大方。

烏衣門第

中国紫檀博物馆
China Red
Sandalwood
Museum

一一〇　中国紫檀博物馆内景

——乌木嵌黄杨云龙纹屏风宝座间

An Interior View of China Red Sandalwood Museum

——A Room of Screen And Throne of Ebony Inlaid with Boxwood with Cloud-Dragon Pattern

一一一 乌木嵌黄杨云龙纹屏风

清式 原件藏故宫博物院

底座 369×33 厘米 通高 306 厘米

A Screen of Ebony Inlaid with Boxwood with Cloud-Dragon Pattern

Ebony And Boxwood

Qing Style The original piece is in the collection of the Palace Museum

◎ 乌木制。屏分三扇，正扇稍宽。采用高浮雕手法雕刻云纹，云纹间施以黄杨木雕刻的苍龙教子图，云纹流畅自然，龙身委婉回旋，尤其是利用乌木与黄杨木色彩的强烈反差，使图案更加生动活泼。屏风下三联底座，屏上三联凤纹屏帽，均施以精美雕刻。

一一二　乌木嵌黄杨云龙纹宝座

清式　原件藏故宫博物院

长 130 厘米　宽 80 厘米　高 120 厘米

A Throne of Ebony Inlaid with Boxwood with Cloud-Dragon Pattern

Ebony And Boxwood

Qing Style　The original piece is in the collection of the Palace Museum

◎ 乌木制。面下带束腰，上下装托腮，拱肩直腿回纹马蹄，下承托泥。左右后三面围子以乌木雕云纹为地，以黄杨木雕龙纹形成强烈反差，极具立体感。扶手及靠背顶端雕福磬及夔龙纹，圆润细腻。

一一三　乌木“仕女图”围屏

清式　单扇长 50 厘米　高 203 厘米　总长 400 厘米

A Folding Screen Decorated with Paintings of *The Noble Beauties*

Ebony

Qing Style

◎ 乌木制。屏分八扇，分五抹界四格，上眉和中腰浮雕拐子纹，下裙板浮雕博古纹。屏风正中绢画仕女图，色调明快，艺术水平颇高。

一一四　乌木棂门圆角柜

明式　长 95 厘米 宽 44 厘米 高 184 厘米

A Tapered Cabinet with Lattice Doors
Ebony
Ming Style

◎ 乌木制。正面对开两门，上棂下板，正中以绦环板相隔。上部以四合如意云纹攒成透棂，工整规矩。门中活动立栓，镶条形面叶。俗称“面条柜”。柜框四角打圆，且侧脚收分明显，俊秀美观。造型特点均属明式。

一一五　乌木平头插肩榫大画案

明式　长 193 厘米 宽 103 厘米 高 81 厘米

A Large Flat Painting Table with Legs in Bridle Joints
Ebony
Ming Style

◎ 乌木制。参照明代紫檀大画案制成。面下长牙板及牙头，插肩榫结构。四腿用料粗壮，有横枨前后连接。

一一六　乌木雕寿字纹长桌

清式　原件藏故宫博物院
长 160 厘米　宽 59 厘米　高 97 厘米

A Long Table Decorated with The Chinese Character *Shou* (Longevity)
Ebony
Qing Style　The original piece is in the collection of the Palace Museum

◎ 乌木制。长条形，面下束腰，下垫托腮。齐牙板上浮雕不同字体的“寿”字 128 个，两端与腿交圈。牙板下附曲边牙条，浮雕“卍”字纹及流苏，方腿回纹马蹄。

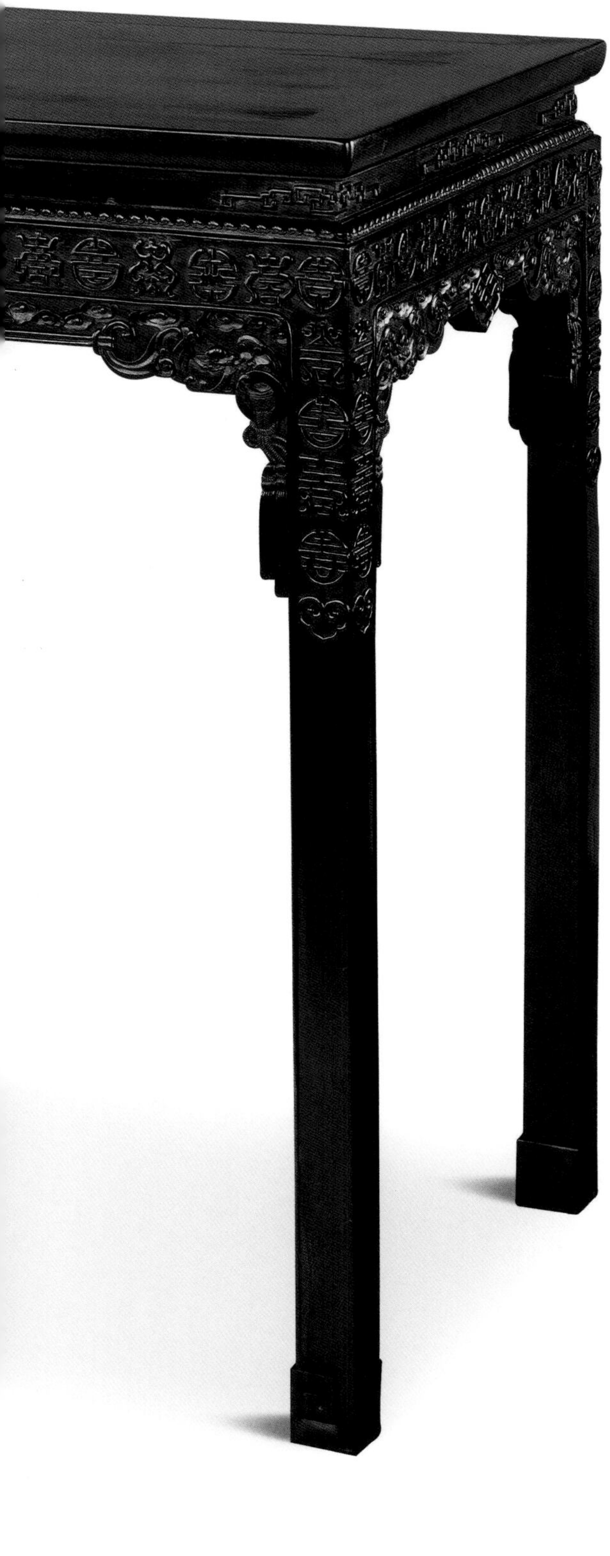

屏風清影

中国紫檀博物馆
China Red
Sandalwood
Museum

一一七　朱家溍为紫檀雕“清明上河图”插屏题跋

座 135×65 厘米 高 176 厘米

Annotation by Mr. Zhu Jiajin for The Red Sandalwood Screen Carved with Images from The Painting *The Festival of Pure Brightness on the River*

◎ 紫檀雕“清明上河图”大插屏由十二块插屏组成，每块插屏长 270 厘米，以木为锦，以雕代笔、以刀作画，运用高浮雕兼镂雕、毛雕、圆雕等技法，生动地再现了宋人张择端所画的“清明上河图”全卷。远山近水、人物牲畜、树石屋瓦，无不惟妙惟肖，立体地再现了当时社会的繁荣景象。该作品由故宫博物院提供原图并监制，朱家溍先生为其题跋。

一一八　紫檀雕“清明上河图”大插屏之一（总十二件）

长 270 厘米　宽 76.5 厘米　高 177 厘米

A Screen Carved with Images from The Painting *The Festival of Pure Brightness on the River* (First out of Twelve Pieces in Total)
Red Sandalwood

一一九　紫檀雕“清明上河图”大插屏之二

长 270 厘米 宽 76.5 厘米 高 177 厘米

A Screen Carved with Images from The Painting *The Festival of Pure Brightness on the River* (Second out of Twelve Pieces in Total)
Red Sandalwood

一二〇　紫檀雕“清明上河图”大插屏之三

长 270 厘米　宽 76.5 厘米　高 177 厘米

A Screen Carved with Images from The Painting *The Festival of Pure Brightness on the River* (Third out of Twelve Pieces in Total)
Red Sandalwood

一二一　紫檀雕“清明上河图”大插屏之四

长 270 厘米 宽 76.5 厘米 高 177 厘米

A Screen Carved with Images from The Painting *The Festival of Pure Brightness on the River* (Fourth out of Twelve Pieces in Total)
Red Sandalwood

一二二　紫檀雕“清明上河图”大插屏之五

长 270 厘米 宽 76.5 厘米 高 177 厘米

A Screen Carved with Images from The Painting *The Festival of Pure Brightness on the River* (Fifth out of Twelve Pieces in Total)

Red Sandalwood

一二三　紫檀雕"清明上河图"大插屏之六

长 270 厘米 宽 76.5 厘米 高 177 厘米

A Screen Carved with Images from The Painting *The Festival of Pure Brightness on the River* (Sixth out of Twelve Pieces in Total)
Red Sandalwood

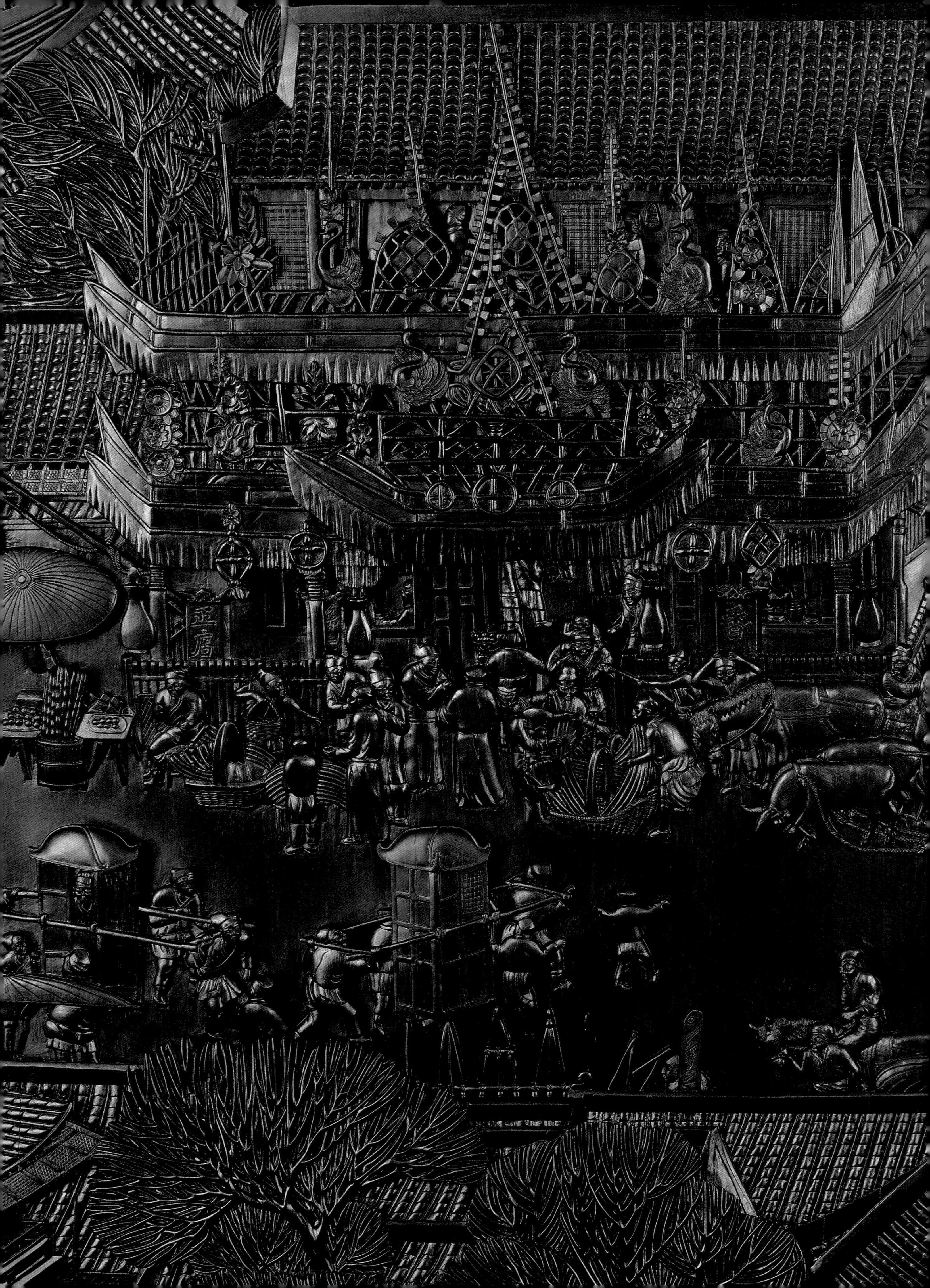

一二四　紫檀嵌檀香雕“清明上河图”插屏之一（总八件）

长 188.5 厘米　宽 50 厘米　高 97 厘米

A Screen of Red Sandalwood Inlaid with Sandalwood with The Painting *The Festival of Pure Brightness on the River* (First out of Eight Pieces in Total)
Red Sandalwood And Sandalwood

◎ 该组作品总计有八件组成。紫檀木边座，底座中间嵌三联绦环板，浮雕拐子纹。前后披水牙，浮雕拐子纹及西洋卷草纹。立柱两侧以站牙夹抵。屏框四边饰混面双边线，框内镶檀香木板心，以高浮雕手法再现了宋代张择端“清明上河图”原貌。雕工细腻，堪称绝品。

一二五　紫檀嵌檀香雕“清明上河图”插屏之二

A Screen of Red Sandalwood Inlaid with Sandalwood with The Painting *The Festival of Pure Brightness on the River* (Second out of Eight Pieces in Total)
Red Sandalwood And Sandalwood

古建余暉

中国紫檀博物馆
China Red
Sandalwood
Museum

一二六　紫檀制天坛祈谷坛·祈年殿（1:10）

An Architectural Model of Qi Nian Dian in Tian Tan (Hall of Praying for Good Harvest in Temple of Heaven)
Red Sandalwood

◎ 祈年殿是天坛祈谷坛的主体建筑，为皇帝祈祷一年风调雨顺、五谷丰登之地。殿宇以“天圆”为平面的基础构思，在三层圆形高大的台基之上，建筑一座有宝顶、三层重檐且层层收缩的圆形攒顶式大殿，是中国古代木结构建筑的经典之作。此作品以原建筑物为准，工艺考究，一丝不苟，每一细微之处的制作都十分精巧。

一二七　紫檀制故宫角楼（1:5）

An Architectural Model of Corner Tower of The Palace Museum
Red Sandalwood

◎ 故宫城墙四隅各耸立角楼一座。角楼由三层屋檐、六个歇山式屋顶、七十二条脊组成，构造繁复，为中国古代建筑中的绝妙神品。这座以紫檀木精心制作的角楼模型，雕刻精细入微，一丝不苟，再现了故宫角楼的风貌。

一二八　紫檀制万春亭（1:5）

An Architectural Model of Ten-Thousand Spring Pavilion
Red Sandalwood

◎ 万春亭位于故宫御花园中，与千秋亭东西相对，且构造相同。亭重檐，上圆下方，取“天圆地方”之意。此作品以原建筑物为准制作而成。

萬春亭

一二九　紫檀制松柏交翠亭（1:5）

An Architectural Model of Pine and Cypress Pavilion
Red Sandalwood

◎ 松柏交翠亭，坐落于北京天安门西侧的中山公园内。公园原为明清两代皇帝祭祀的地方，1914 年辟为中央公园，为纪念孙中山先生，1918 年改名中山公园，后修建此亭。亭原为六角筒瓦凉亭，1930 年换成绿琉璃瓦，改名松柏交翠亭。此作品以珍贵的紫檀为原料，运用手工雕刻技艺，完美地再现了六角亭的原貌。

一三〇　紫檀制飞云楼（1:10）

An Architectural Model of Heavenly Pavilion
Red Sandalwood

◎ 飞云楼位于山西万荣县介店镇，创建于唐贞观年间。此楼外观三层四檐，两层之间设暗层一道，实为五层，四面中心各突出抱厦一间，与楼身拐角相连，抱厦上有斗拱，檐柱与歇山式屋顶，山花向外，最上檐为十字歇山顶，脊中安置宝珠和脊刹。楼上有翼角三十二个，起翘较大。此建筑因独具匠心的构造，被世人称为天下第一楼。此作品以珍贵的紫檀为原料，运用手工雕刻技艺，完美地再现了飞云楼的原貌。

一三一　紫檀制龙泉寺牌坊（1:5）

An Architectural Model of Memorial Gateway at Long Quan Temple
Red Sandalwood

◎ 牌坊是中国传统建筑中极具装饰性的建筑形式。位于山西省五台山的龙泉寺始建于北宋，民国时期（1920–1926）重修时，建成汉白玉雕龙牌坊的脊、梁、柱、基等部位综合运用圆雕、浮雕、透雕等技法，雕刻姿态各异的龙共计320条，构筑巧妙，雕工精湛，世所罕见。此作品以原建筑物为标准，工艺考究，一丝不苟，每一细微之处的制作都十分精巧。

峻凌霄漢
佛光普照
登彼岸

一三二　紫檀制民宅四合院（1:5）

A Detail from The Architectural Model of A Residential Compound with Houses That Surround A Courtyard
Red Sandalwood

◎ 整体紫檀木制。“四合院”作为我国北方民居的一种建筑形式，历史悠久。这座三进院的“四合院”模型，制作规整，完美地再现了中国古建筑的民族风貌。

一三三　紫檀及阴沉木制老北京永定门（1:10）

Yongdingmen
Red Sandalwood And Yinchen Wood

◎ 永定门始建于明嘉靖时期（1521- 1567），由箭楼、城楼和瓮城三部分组成，为老北京城“内九外七”之首。它位于外城南垣正中，为外城正门，规格为外城最高。古时皇帝出京时走此门，有“江山永定”之意。永定门于 1957 年被拆除。为让后人重温老北京城的古风古韵，中国紫檀博物馆馆长陈丽华女士延请名匠，用名贵紫檀木、阴沉木为原料，手工打造老北京城门楼微缩景观，以期还原一个原汁原味的老北京古城风貌。

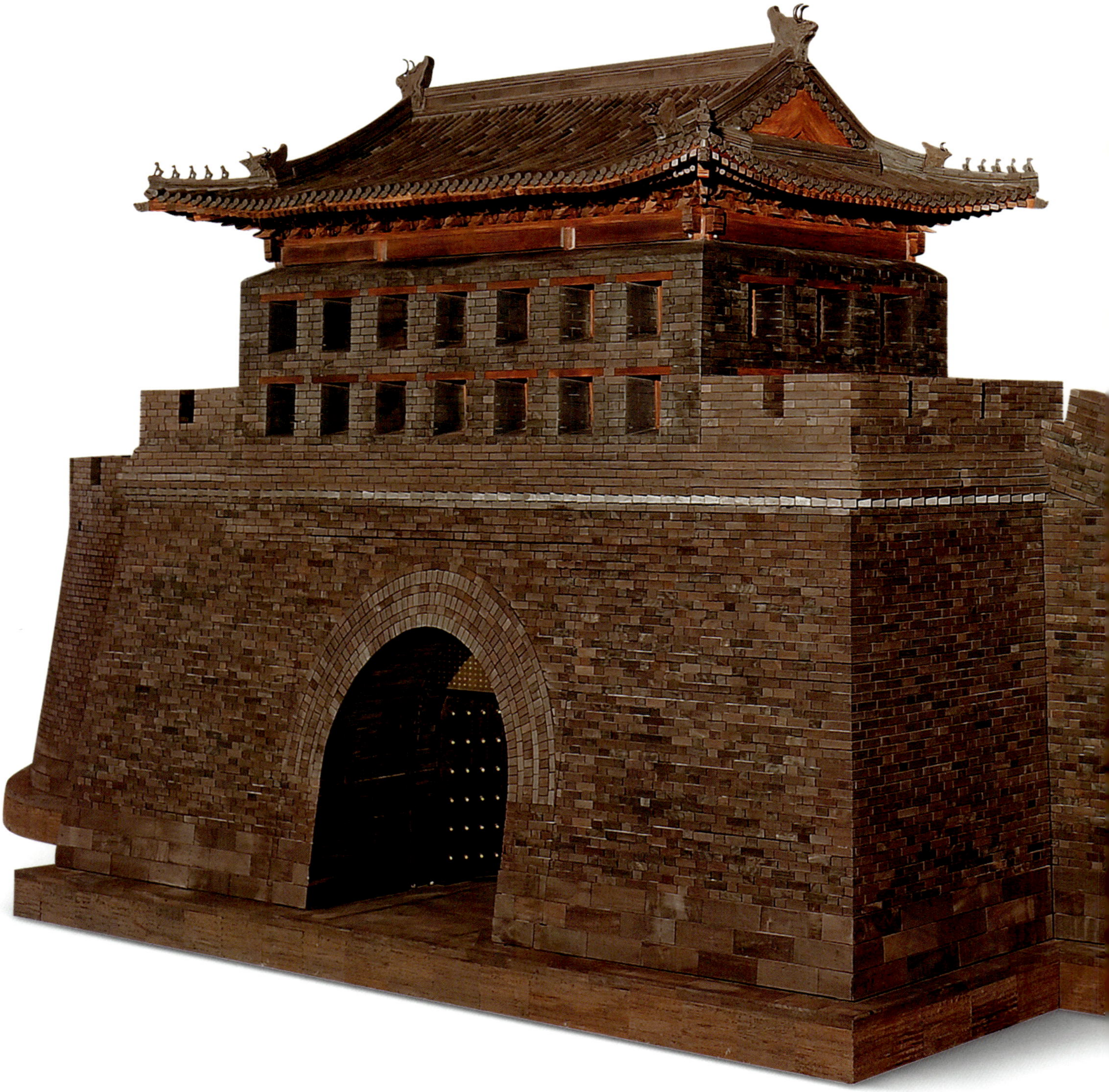

永定門
永定門

匠意玲瓏

中国紫檀博物馆
China Red
Sandalwood
Museum

一三四　中国紫檀博物馆内景

——樟木雕鹤鹿同春落地花罩

An Interior View of China Red Sandalwood Museum

——A Floral Patterned Archway

一三五　中国紫檀博物馆内景

——隔扇

An Interior View of China Red Sandalwood Museum

——Partition Boards

一三六　黄花梨雕荷趣茶托

高 67 厘米

A Tea Tray Set with Lotus Carvings
Huanghuali Wood

一三七　黄花梨雕荷趣画筒

高 83 厘米

A Scroll Hɔlder with Lotus Carvings
Huanghuali Wood

一三八　黄花梨雕龙凤大画筒

底径 90 厘米　高 60 厘米

A Scroll Holder with Dragon And Phoenix Carvings
Huanghuali Wood

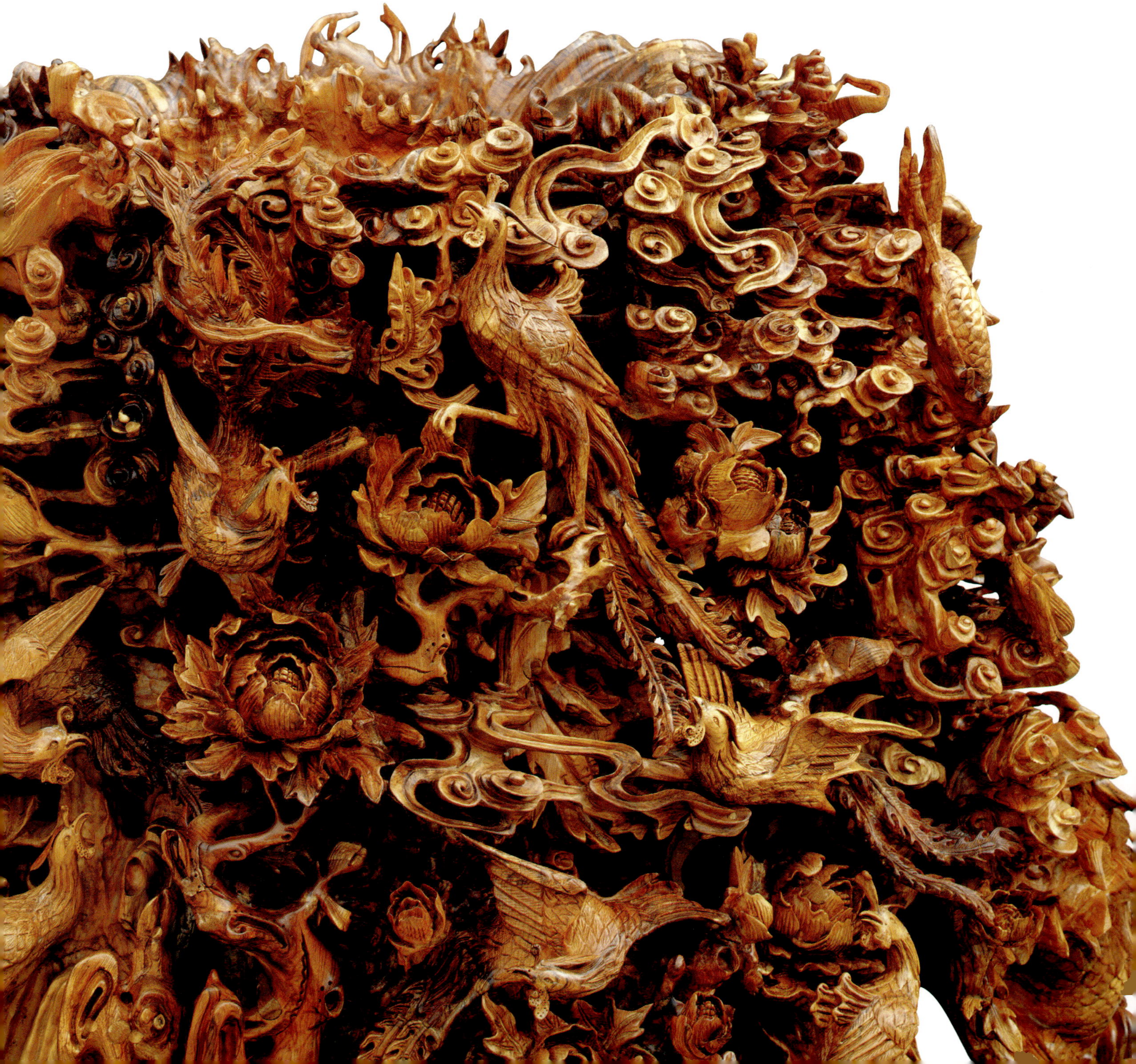

一三九　黄花梨笔筒

明代　径 21.5 厘米 高 20 厘米

A Brush Pot
Huanghuali Wood
Ming Dynasty

一四〇　紫檀雕“松鹤延年”笔筒

径 22 厘米　高 25 厘米

A Brush Pot Carved with The Painting of *Pines and Cranes* (Longevity)
Red Sandalwood

一四一　紫檀雕“喜鹊登梅”笔筒

径 35 厘米 高 38 厘米

A Brush Pot Carved with The painting of *The Magpie on Plum* (Joyful Scene)
Red Sandalwood

一四二　紫檀雕麒麟纹镜匣

长 40 厘米 宽 29 厘米 高 23 厘米

A Cosmetic Chest Carved with *Qilin* (A Chinese Fabulous Animal) Pattern
Red Sandalwood

一四三　紫檀雕博古纹首饰盒

长 45 厘米 宽 31 厘米 高 22 厘米

A Jewellery Box Carved with *Bogu* Pattern
Red Sandalwood

一四四　紫檀嵌象牙雕龙纹如意

长 48 厘米

A Ruyi with Dragon Pattern And Ivory Inlaid
Red Sandalwood And Ivory

一四五　紫檀雕花如意

长 48 厘米

A Ruyi with Floral Patterns
Red Sandalwood

一四六　紫檀边嵌檀香心雕“溪山行旅图”挂屏

清式　宽 52 厘米　高 121.5 厘米

A Wall Panel with Red Sandalwood Frame And Sandalwood Inlaid with Carved Images from The Painting *Travelers, Mountains and Waters*

Red Sandalwood And Sandalwood

Qing Style

一四七　紫檀边嵌檀香心雕“仕女图”挂屏（一对）

清式　宽 40 厘米　高 93.5 厘米

A Pair of Wall Panels with Red Sandalwood Frame And Sandalwood Inlaid with Carved Images from The Painting *The Noble Beauties*
Red Sandalwood And Sandalwood
Qing Style

一四八　中国紫檀博物馆内景

——佛堂

An Interior View of China Red Sandalwood Museum

——A Corner of The Hall of Worshipping Buddha

一四九　紫檀雕花佛龛

长 101.5 厘米　宽 66.5 厘米　高 130.5 厘米

A Niche for A Statue of The Buddha with Floral Pattern
Red Sandalwood

一五〇　黄花梨根雕经幢

高 162 厘米

A Root Carving Banner of Buddhist Scripture
Huanghuali Wood

一五一　黄花梨根雕经幢

高 113 厘米

A Root Carving Banner of Buddhist Scripture
Huanghuali Wood

一五二　樟木根雕“西游记”

底径 140 厘米 高 200 厘米

A Root Carving with The Story of *The Journey to The West*
Camphor Wood

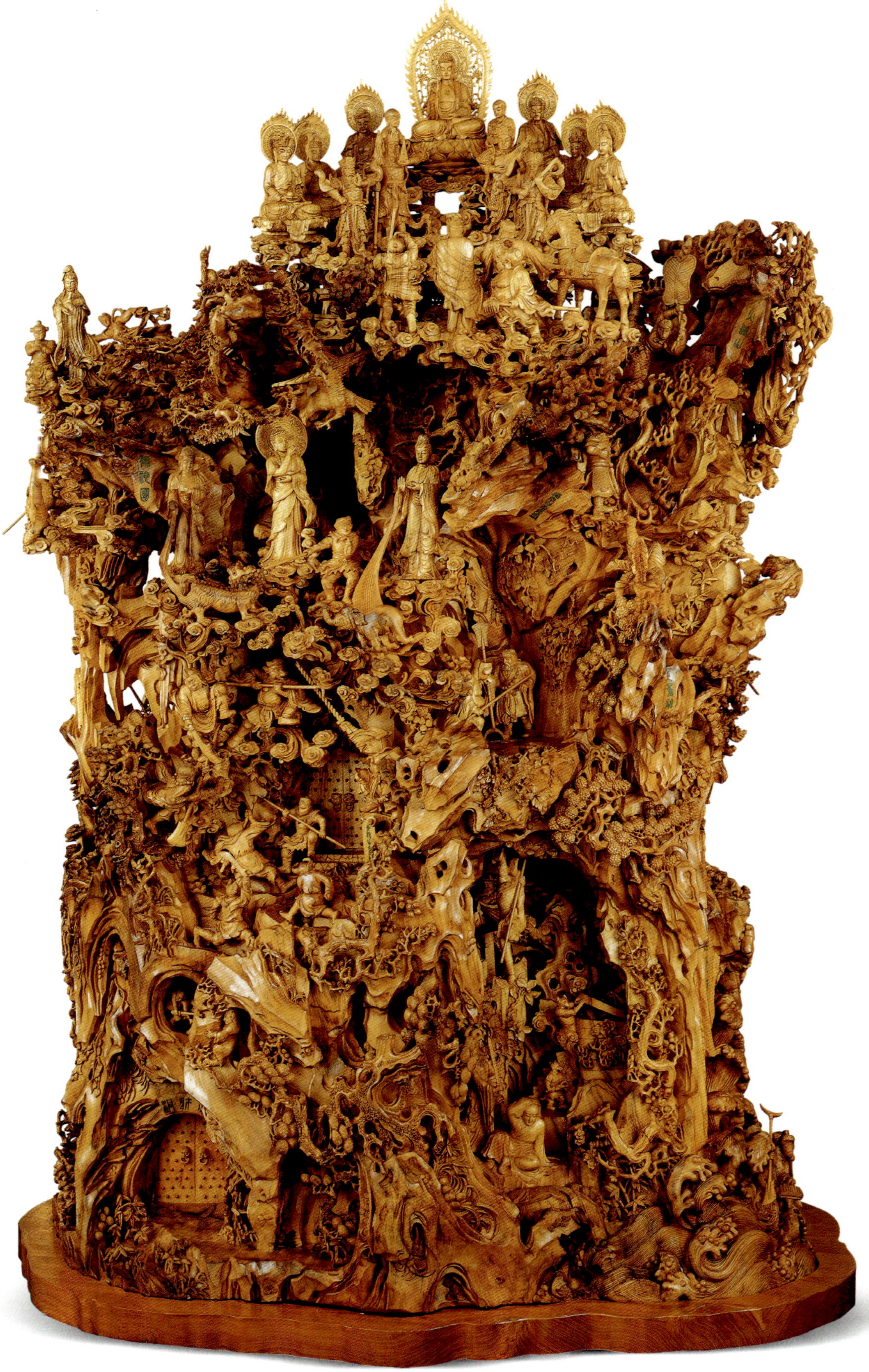

西行取經

赵勇
北京市政协委员
富华国际集团总裁

by Chiu Yung
President of Fu Wah International Group
Member of Beijing Chinese People's Political Consultative Conference

后记

紫檀一直是母亲的梦想，从1976年到2006年，为了这个梦想，母亲付出了三十年的时间，这其中的甘苦滋味只有母亲知道。母亲常常对我们说，紫檀艺术是老祖宗留给我们的宝贝，丢了太可惜了，她要把檀雕这门手艺传下去。她这样说，也这样去做了。三十年来，她对紫檀的痴迷就像王世襄老先生说的那样，达到了忘我的程度。她在紫檀上的付出，也到了倾其所有的地步。作为儿子，除了默默地支持，对母亲似乎不该再有别的什么要求了。

关于这本书，其实已经说了几年时间了，但因为母亲的关系，迟迟没有出版，她说她还是一个学生，还不到出书的时候。其实，这么多年来，一直在母亲身边，看母亲为传承紫檀艺术所作的一切，无论是做人，还是做事，我从母亲那里得到了许多的教益。尤其是近些年，母亲已年近古稀，却还亲自带着紫檀精品远赴美国、日本、韩国和马来西亚等国巡展。在2005年和2006年两年之中，她又出人意料地将中国紫檀博物馆的几件大型紫檀古建模型捐给了世界五大博物馆以作永久收藏。这给我的冲击是很大的，从母亲的这举动中，我感受到紫檀在她的心里，已不仅仅是一种个人爱好了，它早就成为了一种文化，希望让全世界的人拥有。

2006年对母亲来说是值得纪念的一年。三十年，是一段历程的结束，也是一段历程的开始。我觉得这正是一个机会，便极力劝说母亲，这才有了今天这本书的面世。《丽质华堂》是王世襄老先生题的书名，里面融进了母亲的名字“丽华”，“珍贵的材质，华美的殿堂”，说的是紫檀，说的也是母亲亲手建立起来的中国紫檀博物馆，这是对母亲三十年紫檀人生最好的总结和赞誉。

在这本书出版之际，借此机会，我代表我和我的母亲感谢王世襄、文怀沙两位老先生，感谢故宫博物院院长、国家文化部副部长郑欣淼先生，三位在百忙之中，为母亲的第一本书亲自撰文，令我感激之至。感谢国家文物局的老局长张文彬先生，在得知母亲出书的消息后，亲自联系出版单位，商谈相关的出书事宜，感谢文物出版社社长苏士澍先生和出版社的编辑、摄影师，为本书的出版所作的大量工作；感谢故宫博物院的胡德生先生，为该书的展品部分撰写词条说明；感谢中国紫檀博物馆副馆长迟重瑞先生，以及负责此书的相关工作人员，为本书所做的大量方案工作；感谢紫檀制作厂的所有工匠师傅们，是他们的精雕细琢，才有了书中的一件件巧夺天工的珍品。在此，一并向这本书所有的参与者和支持者表示最衷心的感谢！

2006 年末

Postscript

The restoration and manufacture of red sandalwood pieces has always been a long cherished dream of my mother. From 1976 to 2006, my mum has devoted herself to this labor of love. She knows best what she has endured for her beloved red sandalwood. My mother often tells us that red sandalwood art was left by our ancestors and we must not abandon it. She is a woman of her word. As described by Mr. Wang Shixiang, my mother's zeal for the preservation of red sandalwood became a selfless obsession for which she spared no personal expense. As her son, in humble admiration, I offer her my silent support.

Several years ago, someone suggested that my mum publish a book of her own. However, she procrastinated for several years believing that she was still a student and that it was not a prudent time for her own book. In fact, I have been at her side these many years and I have witnessed her determined efforts to pass on red sandalwood art to future generations. I continue to benefit from my mother's wisdom and advice. She is a living example on how to be a person of both integrity and action. In recent years she has withdrawn from the management of Fuwah International Group and thrown her heart and soul into her red sandalwood endeavors. Although she is approaching her seventies she personally brought red sandalwood masterpieces overseas and conducted exhibition tours in the USA, Japan, South Korea and Malaysia. Coming as a surprise, she made donations to the permanent collections of five famous museums in the world in 2005 and 2006. I was shocked by her conduct. However, from this I saw another side of my mum when I realized that red sandalwood was not only her personal love anymore, but had become a kind of culture which she wanted to promote to the rest of the world.

The year 2006 became memorable for my mother. It not only marks the end of a 30 year journey, but also the beginning of a new venture. I believe this is the perfect juncture at which to make the publication of her book a reality. A most befitting title for the book, *Li Zhi Hua Tang*, was proposed by Mr. Wang Shixiang. My mother's name, "Li Hua" is blended into the title. Li Zhi Hua Tang, means Precious Wood and Magnificent Palace. It refers both to the precious red sandalwood and to the palace-like China Red Sandalwood Museum set up by my mother. The title most accurately sums up my mother's life with red sandalwood over the past thirty years and is the most fitting acclamation of her contributions to red sandalwood art.

On the occasion of its publication, on behalf of my mother and me, I wish to offer our gratitude to the many individuals who assisted with this book. We are very appreciative of the advice and expertise offered by the esteemed gentlemen: Mr. Wang Shixiang, an authority on furniture of the Ming and Qing dynasties and

Mr. Wen Huaisha, a master of studies in ancient Chinese civilization. We are extremely grateful to include in this book, articles personally written by Mr. Zheng Xinmiao, director of the Palace Museum and Vice Minister of Culture for PRC. We would also like to sincerely thank Mr. Zhang Wenbin, former director of the State Bureau of Cultural Relics, who personally contacted the publishing house to discuss matters concerning publication. As well, we would like to take this opportunity to express our gratitude to Mr. Su Shiyi, chairman of the Cultural Relics Publishing House and commend the fine work by the editors and photographers. We are indebted to Mr. Hu Desheng, who wrote the explanations for exhibits in the book. Finally, we offer sincere gratitude to Mr. Chi Chungsui, deputy director of the China Red Sandalwood Museum; all relevant working staff for their hard work. We extend a genuine accolade to all the artisans in the red sandalwood manufacturing factory who, with meticulous care, created the wonderful masterpieces shown in this book. Without the companionship, encouragement and support of these and many other fine people this publication could never have become a reality. To all of you, we remain forever grateful.

迟重瑞
中国紫檀博物馆副馆长
北京紫檀文化基金会理事长

Chi Chungsui
Deputy Curator of China Red Sandalwood Museum
Director of China Red Sandalwood Cultural Foundation

檀香沁心　书香盈袖

——《丽质华堂》增订版感言

我出生于一个京剧世家，祖辈五代都是唱京剧的，小时候，家中客厅、卧室中陈设的家俱是用黄花梨制作的——有八仙桌、太师椅、床榻等等。每天放学后，和几个同学一起趴在八仙桌上写作业，嗅着黄花梨的香，望着古典家俱的美，从那时起，我便被中国传统古典家俱那种含蓄、优雅的气质所陶醉，这种美好的景象，至今一直深深地印刻在我的脑海之中。

上世纪八十年代末，在出演了央视八七版《西游记》中的唐僧角色之后，一次偶然的邂逅，我与陈丽华女士相识。由于幼时家庭背景的熏陶，我们都对古典家俱情有独钟。时至今日，我和陈馆长已经共同走过了二十三个春秋。在这些年里，凭着对中国传统古典家俱艺术的一腔热情，从爱好到责任，从制作到传承，一路走来，曾经的酸甜苦辣，让人回味无穷。

紫檀和黄花梨，是中国传统古典家俱中最高级的用材，其木质和油性非常适合用来制作家具和雕刻艺术品。紫檀木产于印度，黄花梨木产于中国海南，是世上现存最为稀少名贵的树种，非千年不能成材。正是由于它的稀有性，让选择和购买紫檀和黄花梨难上加难。为了搜寻到上乘原料，我们跋山涉水，深入密林，在经历重重险阻，最终见到心仪木料的那一刻，感觉一切都释然了，为了自己心爱的紫檀和黄花梨，我们所有的付出和努力都是值得的。

“千淘万漉虽辛苦，吹尽狂沙始到金。”一九九九年九月十九日，中国紫檀博物馆诞生了。作为一家私人博物馆，十二年来，接待了来自世界各地的游客、海外华侨及各国政要，得到了社会各界人士的一致好评。目前，中国紫檀博物馆收藏明清古典家俱精品近千件，馆内每一件作品，都蕴藏着它独特的韵味与涵养——器美、艺精，加上紫檀和黄花梨凝脂玉质般的天然美，在参观游览中，会带给您一种超凡脱俗的视觉享受。通过这些年对宫廷御用家具的研究，我认为，机器生产出的家具只能称为商品，而只有通过传统工艺手工制作的，才能称为艺术品，才更有文化价值。因为，每一件手工雕刻出的艺术作品，体现出的是我们和匠师独到的修养和欣赏品味，饱含着我们对紫檀艺术的痴迷。

从紫檀博物馆开馆至今，我和陈丽华馆长通过在世界各国举办紫檀艺术专题展览和捐赠藏品给国内外知名博物馆等方式，一步一步地实现着我们“让紫檀文化走向世界”的愿望。将馆内的每一件作品完美地展示给全世界，让更多的人近距离地感受中国檀雕艺术的魅力，成为我们促进中外文化交流的一种责任和使命。2011 年 9 月，国务院公布了第三批国家级非物质文化遗产名录项目，中国紫檀博物馆申报的“紫檀雕刻”技艺榜上有名。获此殊荣，不但体现了国家对传统雕刻工艺的重视，也是对我们倾尽心力几十载的一种肯定和认同。

站在书房的窗边，看着院落中的一草一木，望着眼前紫檀博物馆宏伟的身影，不禁感慨万千。二十多年弹指一挥间，在这些年里，为传承檀雕技艺、促进中外文化交流事业，我和陈丽华馆长几乎把全部心血都倾注在紫檀工艺事业上。人生在勤，不索何获？唐玄奘万里取经历经十七年，鉴真大和尚历经十年六次东渡，挫折不断依然坚定不移。这种“人生只做一事又何妨”的精神，不断激励着我们，为自己心爱的紫檀事业一直奋斗下去，无怨无悔。

《丽质华堂》，是中国紫檀博物馆出版的第一本大型图书，也是我们呕心沥血从事紫檀事业的一个总结。此书的再版，离不开一直以来兢兢业业为了博物馆的发展而辛勤努力的员工，更离不开故宫博物院的老前辈和社会各界朋友们的大力支持。未来的路还很长，我们愿和所有热爱紫檀事业的朋友们一起，通过坚持不懈的努力，把檀雕技艺永久地传承下去，让中国紫檀文化发扬光大。

2013 年 5 月

Work for Wood: Wonders in Book Words for The Revision of Palace of Natural Beauty

I was born in a family where five generations before me were engaged in Beijing Opera. I clearly remember that the furniture used in my family, such as "Eight Immortals" tables, Old-fashioned wooden armchairs, beds and couches, were all made of Huanghuali Wood. As a child, I, together with some classmates, used to do homework on the "Eight Immortals" table. With fragrance of Huanghuali Wood lingering and graceful shape of antique furniture in sight, from then on, I have been intoxicated by the sense of beauty in Chinese furniture. Such wonderful memory is still as fresh as ever in my mind.

After I played the role of Monk Xuanzang (the major character in the classical Chinese novel Journey to the West) in Journey to the West, a TV series aired in late 80s of the 20th century, I met Madame Chan Laiwa by a chance encounter. With similar influence exerted by families, both of us hold great affection for antique furniture. Twenty three years have witnessed the joys and sorrows we shared together as a couple. Our passionate love upon antique furniture enabled us to start from interest and then shoulder responsibilities by producing and passing it on to next generations. The course we took, with twists and turns, is very impressive and memorable.

Red sandalwood and Huanghuali Wood, whose xylon and oiliness are very fit for sculptures, are super timber used in Chinese antique furniture. Red sandalwood, native to India and Huanghuali Wood, native to Hainan Province of China are among the rarest existing woods. It is said that it takes a thousand of years for them to grow into useful timber. As a result, it is extremely difficult to choose and purchase favorable ones. Nevertheless, we made arduous journeys, going deep in the jungles and through all sorts of obstacles until the moment we found the superb timber. Such an effort, however, is absolutely worthwhile.

As the saying goes "no pains, no gains". Finally China Red Sandalwood Museum was founded on September 19th, 1999. As a private museum well received by the society, it has received visitors across the world, including oversea Chinese and famous politicians. At present, China Red Sandalwood Museum contains almost 1,000 pieces of antique furniture in Ming and Qing styles. Graceful in shape and superb in timber, each piece brings you an extraordinary visual feast. Having researched in Palace Furniture for years, I believe that the furniture made by machine could only be regarded as commodities; only those handmade in traditional way can be treated as works of art and then present inner cultural value. Furthermore, every single handmade sculpture is filled with sculpturers' unique taste, mastery and passionate love upon red sandalwood art.

Since the opening of China Red Sandalwood Museum, Curator Chan and I have successfully held themed exhibitions of Red Sandalwood Art all over the world and donated some collections to well known museums at home and aboard, step by step realizing our desire to spread Red Sandalwood culture. It has become our mission and responsibility to promote cultural exchanges and showcase our collection worldwide enabling more people to enjoy the Red Sandalwood sculptures on the scene. On September 2011, the State Council published the 3rd National Intangible Culture Heritage List where Red Sandalwood sculptural craft proposed by our museum was included. This honor not only manifested the importance of traditional sculpture craftsmanship attached by the country but also represented the well recognition of our best effort over the past decades.

Looking from the window of study, many thoughts came to my mind at the sight of scene before me especially the magnificent structure of Red Sandalwood Museum. Twenty some – odd years are but a brief moment for Curator Chan and I who have devoted ourselves onto the Red Sandalwood art by preserving sandalwood sculpture craft and promoting cultural exchanges between China and the world. "Of diligence as life is, no gains without pains". To obtain Buddhist scriptures, Monk Xuanzang went through thousands of miles in seventeen years to India; to spread Buddhism, Monk Jianzhen braved all hardships to make his voyage to Japan six times in ten years. Their spirit – one life, one cause, inspires us to keep striving for our beloved Red Sandalwood cause from heart and soul.

As the first comprehensive book published by China Red Sandalwood Museum, "Palace of Natural Beauty" covers our life long dedication to Red Sandalwood art. The second edition of this book will not do without the diligent work by museum staff and the strong support by senior experts from the Palace Museum as well as friends of all walks of life. With a long way ahead, we, together with all friends who love Red Sandalwood art, will continue to preserve and promote the Red Sandalwood craft and will pass it down from generations to generations on.

2013.5

Contents

Traditional Royal Furniture Made of Red Sandalwood

Traditional Royal Furniture Made of Jinsinan Wood

Traditional Royal Furniture Made of Ebony

Slidable Screens of *Riverside Scene at Qing Ming Festival*

Afterglow of Ancient Architecture

Ingenious Design And Exquisite Craftsmanship

麗質華堂

中国紫檀博物馆

陳麗華收藏